A Quilted Christmas

A Quilted Christmas

Landauer Publishing, www.landauerpub.com, is an imprint of
Fox Chapel Publishing Company, Inc.

Project Team
Acquisitions Editor: Amelia Johanson
Editor: Jeremy Hauck
Copy Editor: Christa Oestreich
Designer: Wendy Reynolds
Proofreader & Indexer: Jean Bissell

Shutterstock used: Vjom (garland, front cover); sunwart (snowflakes, used throughout); Varts (12); Niccolo Bertoldi (13).

ISBN 978-1-63981-110-6

Library of Congress Control Number: 2025936107

To learn more about the other great books from Fox Chapel Publishing, or to find a retailer near you, call toll-free at 800-457-9112 or visit us at www.FoxChapelPublishing.com.
You can also send mail to:
Fox Chapel Publishing
903 Square Street
Mount Joy, PA 17552

We are always looking for talented authors.
To submit an idea, please send a brief inquiry to acquisitions@foxchapelpublishing.com.

Printed in China
First printing

MIX
Paper | Supporting responsible forestry
FSC® C016973

A Quilted Christmas

16
Projects to Bring the Warmth of the Season Home

Deb Grogan

Landauer Publishing

Contents

J
Y
28

36

44

All is Calm
Silent Night
52

Introduction

December 24, 1958. Four o'clock in the afternoon to be exact—the day and time I was born. So, it shouldn't come as any surprise that my favorite holiday is Christmas. I am delighted by the joys of the season: classic Christmas music, the sound of bells jingling, the smell of cinnamon and nutmeg coming from the kitchen, and decorating the house for celebrations with family and friends.

I want the joy and spirit of the season to fill my home for as long as possible, which is why I begin decorating for the holidays right after Thanksgiving. I love being able to decorate with the projects I have created in this book, along with other cherished trimmings.

I have a penchant for deep cherry reds, creamy whites, and the rich, verdant greens that are so closely associated with the traditional holiday color scheme. In this book, I've used those classic hues of red, green, and white in basic collections, so you can recreate that same timeless look in your own home. However, feel free to choose color combinations that suit your décor and personal style.

The projects in this book are designed to be both easy and enjoyable. From creating and decorating with fun ornaments and banners to welcoming guests with a handmade wall hanging, setting the scene for holiday meals, cozying up by the fire, and ending the day with sweet dreams, there's something for every moment. My hope is that these projects will help you create lasting memories and traditions of your own.

Thank you for joining me. Let's make some memories together!

A NOTE FROM DEB

Writing this book was a heartfelt project for me. I believe traditions are important, and in our fast-paced lives, it's easy to lose sight of them. Through these simple and fun projects, I hope to help you create lasting traditions of your own. Thank you for letting me share my love of quilting with you. It's because of you that I get to do what I love most—create beautiful quilts.

The Tools You'll Need

The tools listed here give you the foundation for a successful quilting project, helping ensure precision, efficiency, and quality in your work.

Basic Tools

Rotary Cutter: This tool allows you to cut fabric quickly and accurately. It's essential for making the clean, straight cuts needed in quilting. Find one that is comfortable for you to use and does not cause hand strain; there are many ergonomic brands on the market. My personal choice is Martelli.

Cutting Mat: A self-healing cutting mat protects your work surface and provides a grid for accurate measuring and cutting. It's a must-have when using a rotary cutter.

Quilting Rulers: Quilting rulers help measure and cut fabric with precision. They come in various sizes and shapes, making it easier to cut straight lines, angles, or specific shapes needed for blocks. I stick to one brand because markings can vary between brands, and I find consistency prevents cutting errors.

Sewing Machine: While quilts can be made by hand, a sewing machine speeds up the process and ensures even stitching. A machine with a walking foot attachment can be especially helpful for quilting the layers together. I recommend a machine that includes certain basic stitches (see page 14) for appliqué.

TIP: Machines with a setting to automatically lift your presser foot, or a stop-with-needle-down option, are recommended. It's not a must, but it's very helpful.

Machine Foot: The best foot to use is an open-toe foot. It allows you to see and guide your stitches around the edge of your appliqué shape.

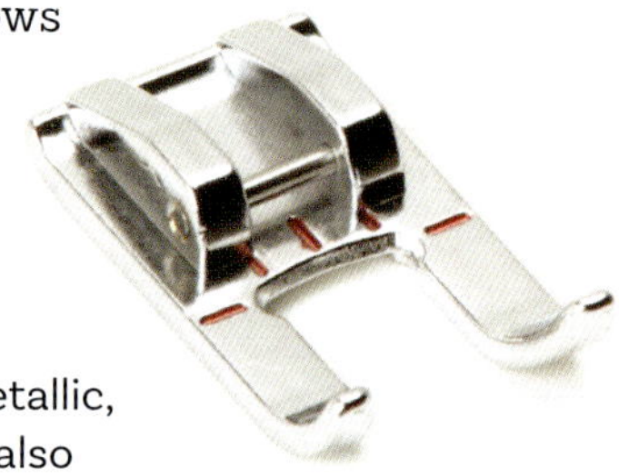

Machine feet are typically metallic, as shown here. But there are also clear acrylic versions that help with seeing your work.

Machine Needles: It is always best to use needles that are recommended for your machine. The most popular sizes for appliqué are 70/10, 75/11, and universal 80/12. The larger the needle, the larger the hole it will put in your fabric while applying your appliqué to your quilt. This matters more if you are using a satin stitch, as that look is created by using a zigzag stitch adjusted so the stitches are very close together. With large needles, you run the risk of creating a perforation along the appliqué shape's edge with needle holes, and the quilt top coming apart. So, be mindful of the needle size and how close the satin stitches are to each other. The needle size will also be determined by the thread you use.

Thread: Thread brands, weights, and colors are plentiful and everyone has their favorites. The first question you need to ask yourself is what look you want your appliqué to have. Do you want the stitches to show? Be only slightly noticeable? Or fade into the design completely? A thread weight of 100 will blend into the fabric—it is ultrathin and makes the stitches

Thread comes in every color you can imagine. You may want to pick a color that matches your work, or one that stands out!

CHOOSING THREAD COLORS

In most cases you would choose a thread that matches the dominant color of your appliqué fabric. Or use a thread color that makes it easier to see the stitches. For a complete tutorial on mastering appliqué stitching, this QR code will take you to my video instructions.

scan for more information

barely noticeable—whereas a heavier thread weight of 40 or 50 can be used to highlight the decorative stitching. Polyester threads are shinier than rayon and stronger than cotton. I prefer an 80-weight poly or rayon, as I tend to do a bit more satin stitch on frequently washed projects.

Bobbin threads should always be the same weight as your top thread. Some people prefer to have both threads be the same color, but I personally prefer a neutral color for my bobbin and change out the top thread to match my work. I never have an issue with thread pull-through showing, but it can be one if your tension is off even a little or the thread weights are not the same. If you do not have same-weighted threads for both bobbin and top, try putting the lighter-weight thread in the bobbin. As always, consult your machine's manual if you have any issues with your tension or speak to your sewing machine dealer.

Iron and Ironing Board: Pressing seams flat is important for accuracy and a clean finish. A good steam iron helps set seams and fabric, making it easier to assemble blocks accurately. Using an ironing board or table set to the correct height for you will reduce arm fatigue and back strain.

Pins and Clips: Pins and clips are used to hold fabric pieces together when sewing. They help ensure layers stay aligned, especially when piecing blocks or assembling the quilt sandwich (top, batting, and backing). I prefer double fork pins for piecing my quilt tops. Especially when nesting seams together, I find these pins hold the seams in place better. I am a pinner. Some people are not, but I prefer pins for accuracy.

Fabric Scissors and Paper Scissors: Good-quality fabric scissors are essential for cutting fabric, trimming edges, or making small cuts that a rotary cutter might not manage. Having a separate pair just for fabric ensures they stay sharp. Then, keep an older pair to use with paper. I prefer scissors with fine serrated edges for cutting out appliqué shapes: they grip the fabric edge better and help produce a nice clean cut. I like to keep a few sizes on hand and prefer the Karen Kay Buckley scissors in small and medium.

Seam Ripper: Mistakes are inevitable, and a seam ripper allows you to easily undo seams without damaging the fabric. It's an essential tool for fixing errors.

Quilting Needles (Hand and Machine): Quilting needles are designed to handle multiple layers of fabric and batting. Machine needles are used for sewing the pieces together, while hand needles are needed for hand quilting or binding.

Marking Tools (Fabric Chalk, Pens, or Pencils): Marking tools are used to draw guidelines for cutting or quilting. Make sure to use ones that are designed for fabric and that can be easily removed or washed out.

Mechanical pencils create a nice crisp, clean line when tracing your templates onto your fusible web. Quilt markers are great for making marks on your fabric that will need to be removed afterward. There are markers that wash out of fabric with water or fade away when heat is applied with an iron. I prefer the kind that wash out. These can lose their sharp point after several uses so I keep extra on hand. I like to have a white quilt pencil and a darker one as well. They look and draw like a colored pencil but wash or rub out of fabrics.

TIP: Use a white quilt pencil to outline the appliqué on a dark background fabric. This makes it easier to see the edge while guiding the machine needle.

NOTE

- For all projects, the yardage listed is based on 42" (106.7cm) usable inches unless otherwise indicated.
- WOF = width of fabric
- HST = half-square triangle
- RST = right sides together
- Fat Eighth = precut fabric, measuring 9" x 22" (22.9 x 55.9cm)

Basting Tools (Safety Pins or Basting Spray): When layering the quilt sandwich (top, batting, and backing), you need to secure the layers together before quilting. Safety pins or basting spray help keep the layers in place, preventing shifting or bunching during the quilting process.

Batting: This is the middle layer of the quilt that provides warmth and softness. There are various types, like cotton, polyester, or wool, and each provides different levels of warmth and loft.

Environment, Posture, and Breaks: While these are not tools, they certainly are important. Your chair should be at the correct height for you. Your arms should rest on the table in front of you with your elbows at a 90-degree angle. Your feet should sit flat on the floor. A chair with good back support and a comfortable seat will make it easier to sew for longer periods. I have a tendency to hunch my shoulders while working, so I make sure to take breaks to stretch or walk around or grab a snack. Keep drinks and food away from your sewing area to prevent unwanted mishaps. Try moving your cutting and ironing stations away from the machine so you need to get up to use them. Your room and the area around the machine should be well lit. I prefer 6500K bulbs in all my studio lighting—that way, my studio lighting mimics daylight. It's also helpful when working with colors.

Appliqué Tools

In all honesty, appliqué could be done with just fabric, scissors, a pencil, and a glue stick, but what fun would that be? Having a few modern tools can make our tasks easier, yield better results, and make appliqué more fun.

Quilting Gloves: I wear a quilting glove on my left hand while doing appliqué, but not on my right hand (your dominant hand will be busy guiding the bulk of the project through the harp). Having a glove on your nondominant hand helps you keep better control of the fabric as you guide the needle around the edge of your appliqué shape. I love the Machingers by Handi Quilter.

Fusible Web: Fusible provides the ability to fuse fabric together. It is usually a soft, sheer web-like material with a paper backing and is heat activated. It can come packaged in sheets of various sizes, as well as on a roll or by the yard. There are some fusible sheets that you can run through your home printer, so you do not have to hand trace the templates; however, with these, you are limited to US letter paper in terms of size.

TIP: If you don't use gloves on a regular basis for general quilting, buy a pair that can be used on either hand. That way, you will always have an extra glove to work with.

There are several brands of fusible web on the market and people have their preferences. If you are new to appliqué, try some different brands to see which one you like. I prefer fusible web that has a softer hand for things like quilts for the bed or throws, and one that is slightly stiffer for wall hangings.

Learn more about fusibles by scanning this QR code.

scan for more information

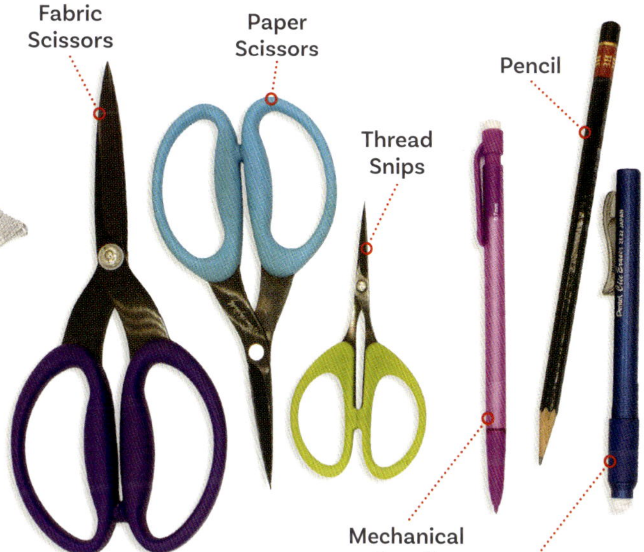

Certain tools make everything easier, so I recommend getting quilting gloves, different types of scissors, and marking tools.

A light pad is a smaller, more lightweight alternative to the light table.

Light Table: A light table will make it easier to trace your templates as well as fuse shapes in place. I prefer a flat one that has variable light levels. Buy the biggest one you can afford, or make one if you are the crafty type. For tracing templates, taping them to a sunny window works just as well.

Spray Starch: Starch helps reduce fraying on the fabric's edge and stiffens it slightly, making it easier to work with.

Glue Sticks: Glue sticks are great for areas where fusible has failed or is missing. Glue sticks are water soluble and will wash out. Fusible can be delicate and may tear if it's separated from the fabric, or if it is not fused completely to the fabric. If the backing paper is not all the way off the fusible, you can try to reheat it with an iron to get it to adhere. The glue stick can fix any areas not fused to the fabric.

Freezer Paper: Freezer paper is great for stabilizing and cutting appliqué shapes out of fabrics that you do not want to use fusible on. They can be regular quilting cottons, or specialty fabrics like felt or wool. I find it especially helpful when trying to cut small pieces.

Stabilizer: Stabilizer is used to prevent the edges of the background fabric around the appliqué from "puckering." Stabilizer is first placed on the back of the area to be appliquéd. A variety of stabilizer products are available, like iron-on, wash-away, and paper tearaway. However, the best one to use for appliqué, I find, is a paper tearaway. As the name applies, once you have finished stitching, you simply tear away the stabilizer from the back of your project. This is especially helpful for lightweight fabrics. For heavier fabrics, you may not need stabilizer. It is always best to test the materials you plan to use.

Learn more about stabilizers by scanning this QR code.

scan for more information

Embroidery Tools

Hand embroidery is a simple and versatile craft that doesn't require many materials and allows for a wide range of creative possibilities. For this book, we are using hand embroidery to embellish and add detail to a few of our projects. But first you'll need the right tools, and you'll need to know the techniques involved.
You don't need many tools, but having the right ones can make the process smoother.

Embroidery Hoop: An embroidery hoop keeps your fabric taut while you work, helping you maintain even stitches. They come in various sizes and are made of wood or plastic. Choose a size that fits your projects.

Embroidery Needles: Embroidery needles have a sharp point and a slightly larger eye to accommodate embroidery floss than regular sewing needles. Choose a needle size based on the thickness of your thread, and the type of fabric you will be embroidering—larger needles for thicker threads, smaller for finer work. My personal choice is a size 8.

Basic embroidery supplies include floss, needles, a needle threader, and a hoop.

Embroidery Floss: Embroidery floss is the thread you'll be stitching with, and it usually comes in six-strand skeins, which can be separated for finer stitching or used together for thicker lines. For finer detail, use one strand, or for bolder lines, two to three strands are most commonly used. Floss is available in a wide variety of colors. Popular brands include DMC and Cosmo. Pearl cotton is a single-strand embroidery thread that can also be used. An 8 weight is equivalent to three strands of regular floss.

Embroidery Scissors: Small, sharp embroidery scissors make it easy to snip threads close to the fabric. Look for ones with sharp points to get into tight spaces.

Water-Soluble Pen or Fabric Marker: You'll want a water-soluble pen or fabric marker for marking your design on the fabric before stitching. The marks can be washed away once you're done. Heat-erasable pens work well, depending on your fabric and preferences.

Thimble: A thimble protects your finger while pushing the needle through thick fabrics or multiple layers. If you're working with thicker fabrics or find the needle difficult to push, this can save your fingers!

Needle Threader: A needle threader helps you thread the needle easily. It's not essential, but it can save time, particularly if you're working with small needle eyes.

Pincushion: A pincushion keeps needles and pins organized while you work.

Appliqué Basics

Appliqué is the art of applying a fabric shape to a larger piece of fabric to create a pattern or design. It is one of my favorite quilting techniques. As an artist, I can recreate designs from my portfolio of art or draw new designs. I love to create appliqué designs that tell a story. If you find appliqué to be a little bit of a challenge, it can also be so much fun if you learn some of the tips and tricks. As I always say, it's just fabric: play, practice, and learn.

Machine Stitches

Some sewing machines have more bells and whistles than a NASA spacecraft, but most appliqué is done with only a few types of stitches: a **blanket stitch**; a **satin stitch**, which is a zigzag stitch with length and width adjusted to push stitches closer together; and a **straight stitch**. You can also use any decorative stitches you may have on your machine. If you use a decorative stitch other than the ones listed, make sure the stitch will cover most of the appliqué shape's edge.

If you are new to appliqué—practice, practice, practice! Use some scrap fabric to cut out a variety of shapes with fusible, layer them on another scrap piece, and practice different stitches, widths, and lengths. Start on the straight edge of the shape and appliqué pieces

DECORATIVE STITCHES

If your machine has decorative stitches, have some fun using scraps and experiment with them. Scan the QR code to watch a quick video on best practices when using decorative stitches in appliqué.

scan for more information

Blanket stitches let the raw edge of the fabric show, even if part of the stitch rests along the top.

Satin stitch are tight vertical lines that create a concealed edge along the fabric.

Straight stitch will leave a raw edge on the appliqué shape.

under an overlap first, and practice pivoting your needle when going around curves. When I find a stitch setting I like, I mark it down on an index card I keep in my sewing drawer, so I always have my preferred settings on hand. You can also use the "save setting" feature on your machine. You don't need a fancy machine to do beautiful appliqué work either; a machine that just has a straight stitch will also work beautifully.

If the quilt you are making will be used frequently and washed, think hard about the decorative stitch you are using. Will the shapes hold up around the edges with multiple washes, or will it fray? I usually use a satin stitch for a project that will be washed frequently, like a table runner or placemat.

TIP: Be careful not to choose a decorative stitch and thread that will overpower a delicate design.

Fusible Web

1. Trace the template on the smooth, paper side of the fusible web.

2. Trim away any excess fusible. Fuse the template (web side) to the wrong side of the appliqué fabric with heat from the iron.

3. Cut out the shape, remove the paper backing, and place the shape on the background fabric. Gently apply the iron to the tops of the shapes. Do not run the iron back and forth; instead, lift the iron and set it down on the next area to be fused. Fuse according to the manufacturer's directions.

4. Place a piece of tearaway stabilizer under the background fabric of the appliqué before stitching.

5. Using your stitch of choice, appliqué the shape to the background fabric.

TIP: If you have one, use an old iron to apply the fusible to the fabric. The fusible can and usually will get on your iron, but it can easily be cleaned off with a magic cleaning sponge. This works best when used on a warm iron. I keep a magic cleaning sponge near my iron at all times and clean the iron frequently when working on a project.

Stabilizer

These steps continue from where Fusible Web (above) leaves off.

6. Here is a completed appliqué. Now it's time to remove the tearaway stabilizer from step 4. First, flip it over.

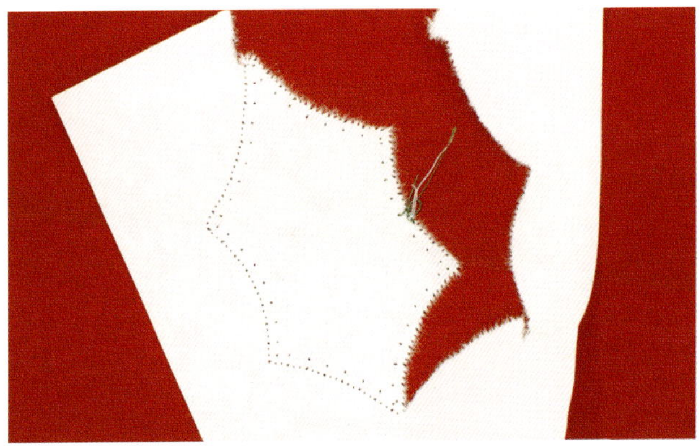

7. Using a seam ripper or the edge of a pair of scissors, make a small slit in the tearaway in the middle and gently pull the stabilizer away from the stitching line.

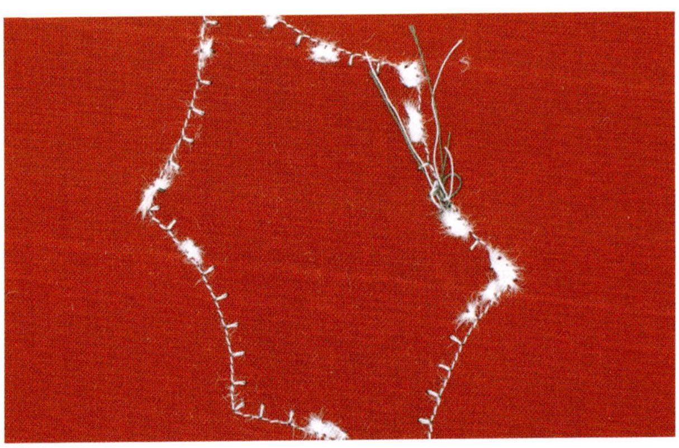

8. Remove as much as you can, but don't worry about smaller bits, as they will disintegrate when washed.

TIP: To remove tearaway, lay the project on a flat surface and use one hand to support the fabric and one to pull the stabilizer away from the project. This helps to support the stitches.

TIP: When using a satin stitch, don't worry about the small line of tearaway that stays underneath the stitches. It is a soft-pulp paper and washes away with time.

Techniques

Half-Square Triangles

Half-square triangles (HSTs) are a handy technique used throughout this book. I prefer the Magic 8 Method, in which you are able to sew, cut, and make eight HST units at one time.

1. Place two squares RST. Here, they are shown as Fabrics A and C. With a light pencil or water-soluble quilt marker, draw a diagonal line from one corner to the other, then the two remaining corners.

2. Sew a seam ¼" (6.4mm) to the left of the drawn line, then ¼" (6.4mm) to the right. Repeat for the other drawn line.

3. Press then cut into four squares. Cut the squares in half on the drawn lines.

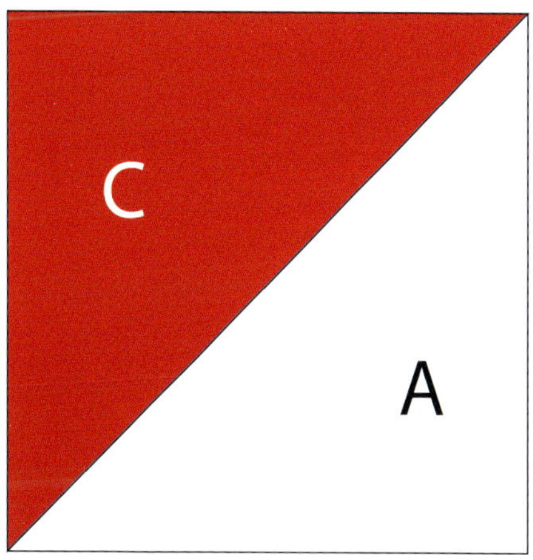

4. Press open and trim. Finger press HSTs open first because they are cut on a bias and can become skewed.

Essential Embroidery Stitches

Hand embroidery is the process of decorating fabric by hand, using a needle and thread. It involves stitching patterns or designs directly onto fabric using basic stitches. Here's a quick guide to some of the most common hand embroidery stitches: back stitch, running stitch, French knot, and satin stitch.

BACK STITCH

The back stitch is great for outlining shapes and creating clean, solid lines.

> **TIP:** Keep the stitches even for a smooth, continuous line.

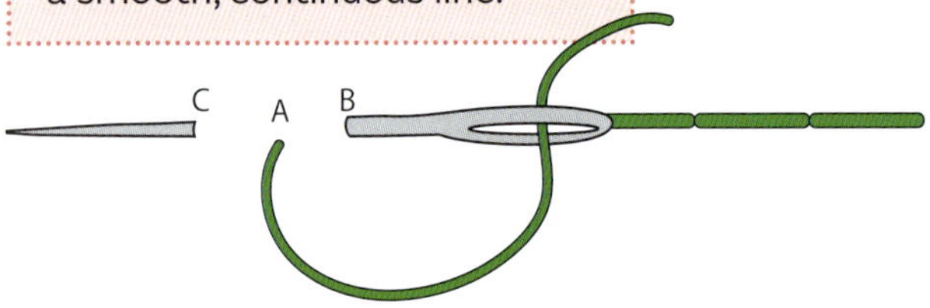

1. Thread the needle and tie a knot at the end.

2. Bring the needle up through the fabric at point **A** (the starting point on the line).

3. Insert the needle down at point **B** (a small distance behind), then bring it up again at point **C** (a stitch-length away from **A**).

4. Insert the needle back into point **A** and pull it through. This creates the first back stitch.

5. Continue, bringing the needle up a stitch-length forward from **C**, and stitch back into point **C**.

RUNNING STITCH

The running stitch is a simple stitch that looks like dashed lines, and it's great for adding texture or creating outlines.

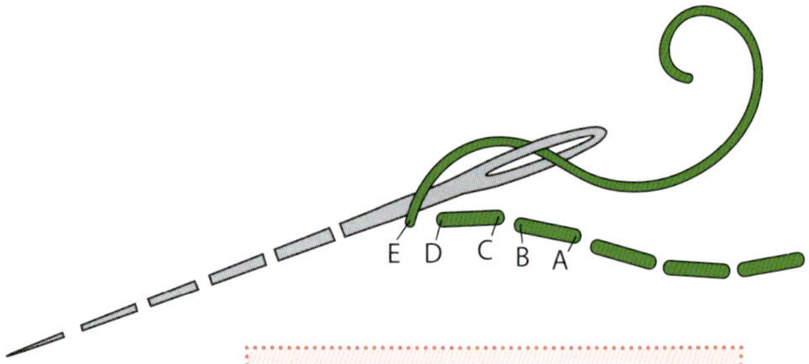

> **TIP:** You can vary the length of the stitches depending on your design.

1. Bring the needle up at point **A**.

2. Insert the needle down at point **B** (a short distance forward), then up at point **C**.

3. Repeat, stitching down at point **D** and up at point **E**, creating a dotted line effect.

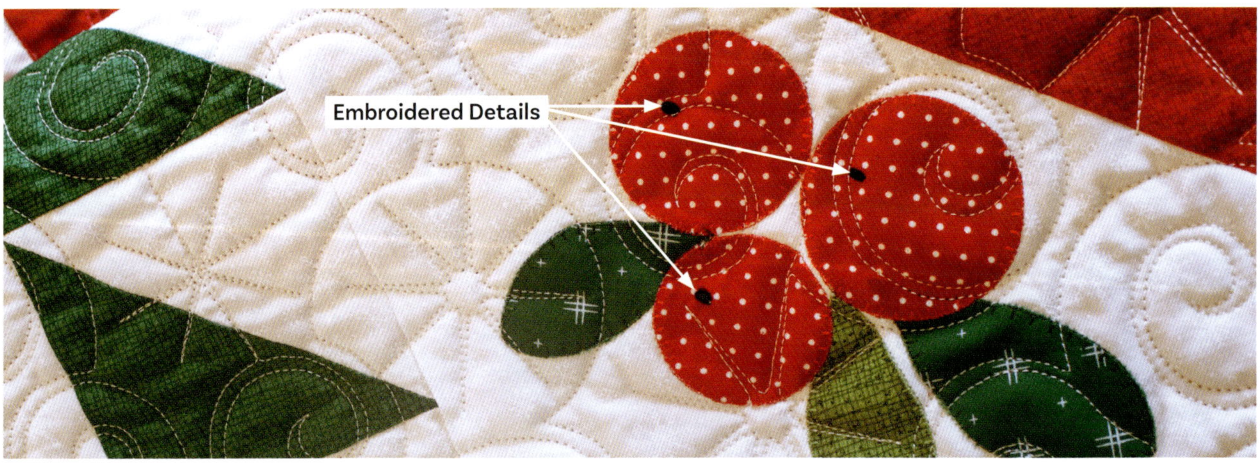

French knots or satin stitch can be used in Home for the Holidays (page 44) to add detail to the holly berries.

FRENCH KNOT

A French knot adds lovely little raised dots, perfect for eyes, flower centers, or decorative details.

> **TIP**: The more wraps, the bigger the knot. Keep the tension even for a neat knot.

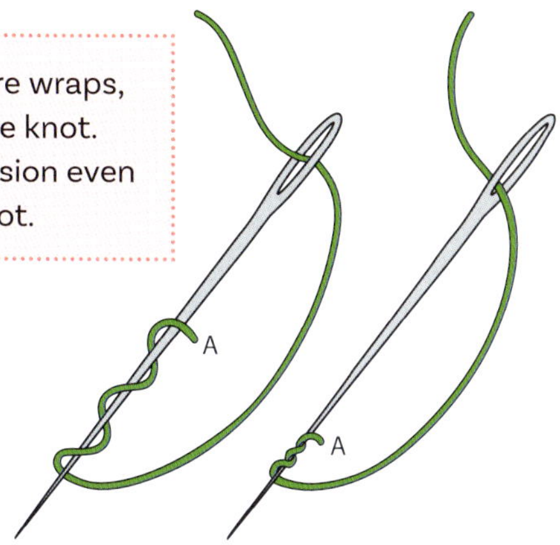

1. Bring the needle up through the fabric at point **A**.

2. Hold the thread taut with one hand. With the other hand, wrap the thread around the needle two to three times.

3. While holding the wraps snugly, insert the needle back into the fabric very close to point **A** (not in the exact same hole, to avoid pulling the knot through).

4. Pull the needle through, keeping gentle tension on the thread as the knot tightens.

> **TIP**: When using the satin stitch, a thin marker in the same color can be used to "fill in" the shape you plan to embroider. This helps prevent any background between the stitches from showing through. This technique is especially helpful when embroidering eyes or small parts.

SATIN STITCH

The satin stitch is a simple and easy way to fill in shapes with solid blocks of color. It creates smooth, satin-like embroidery by placing stitches closely together.

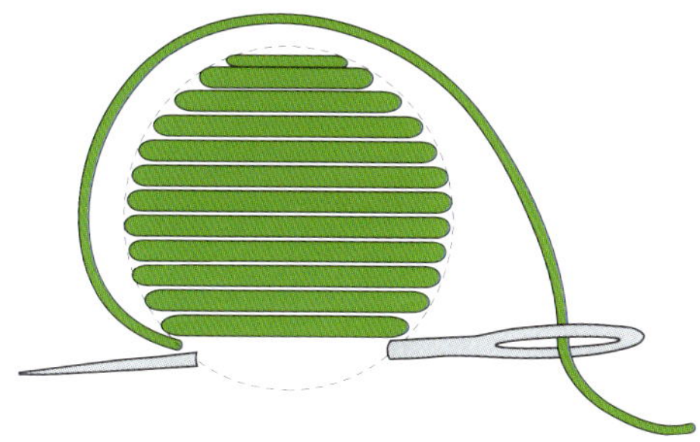

1. Before starting, you may want to outline the area you'll be filling in, either with a back stitch or by drawing the shape lightly with a fabric marker.

2. Bring the needle up from the back of the fabric at one edge of the shape.

3. Insert the needle down directly across from the starting point on the opposite edge of the shape. The stitch should span the entire width of the shape you're filling in.

4. Bring the needle up again right next to where the first stitch started. Repeat, placing each stitch closely alongside the previous one. The goal is to keep the stitches snug without overlapping.

5. Maintain even tension throughout to prevent puckering or loose stitches. This helps create a smooth, glossy surface.

6. Continue this process until the entire area is filled with neat, parallel stitches. When you're done, secure the thread on the back of the fabric.

Winter Friends

Made by Anne Bessette, Madeline Harris, and Deb Grogan.

At the heart of holiday decorating, the Christmas tree is a timeless symbol of joy, togetherness, and festive spirit. Bring a touch of whimsy to your Christmas tree with these adorable felt and fabric ornaments. Each design is full of character, from a cheerful bear bundled in a festive scarf to a wise owl and a playful fox, all ready to celebrate the season. These handmade ornaments are sure to bring joy for years to come.

The ornaments finish at 4½" x 4½" (11.4 x 11.4cm).

TOOLS & MATERIALS

- Winter Friends templates (pages 62–65)
- 1 yard (91.4cm) lightweight fusible web of choice, usually 18" (45.7cm) wide
- Roll of freezer paper
- 6" x 36" (15.2 x 91.4cm) light green felt
- 6" x 36" (15.2 x 91.4cm) medium green felt
  - (4) 6" x 6" (15.2 x 15.2cm) squares, for snowman and fox ornaments
  - 4" x 4" (10.2 x 10.2cm) square, for small holly leaves
- 6" x 36" (15.2 x 91.4cm) red felt
- 5" x 5" (12.7 x 12.7cm) assorted textural and tonal prints in the following colors:
  - (5) white, (2) medium green, (2) dark green, (3) red, (1) very pale pink), (2) medium brown, (1) medium rust, (1) light gray
- 4" x 4" (10.2 x 10.2cm) pale pink felt square, for cheeks
- 4" x 4" (10.2 x 10.2cm) orange felt square, for nose and owl beak
- 4" x 4" (10.2 x 10.2cm) black felt square, for noses
- Stylus
- 1 yard (91.4cm) red satin ribbon, ¼" (6.4mm) wide; cut into (6) 6" (15.2cm) pieces; for small bow
- 1¼ yards (114.3cm) red grosgrain ribbon, ⅝" (1.6cm) wide; cut into (6) 7" (17.8cm) pieces; for hanger
- (18) ¼" (6.4mm) red buttons, for holly berries
- (12) ⅛" (3.2mm) black buttons, for eyes
- Hand needle and thread
- Black embroidery floss
- Small bag of polyfil stuffing
- Red embroidery floss

Making the Ornaments

1. Trace the templates for each ornament, except the small holly leaves, onto the freezer paper. Follow the templates for quantities and colors. Fuse each part to the coordinating fabrics, then cut them out. Do not remove the paper backs until ready to use.

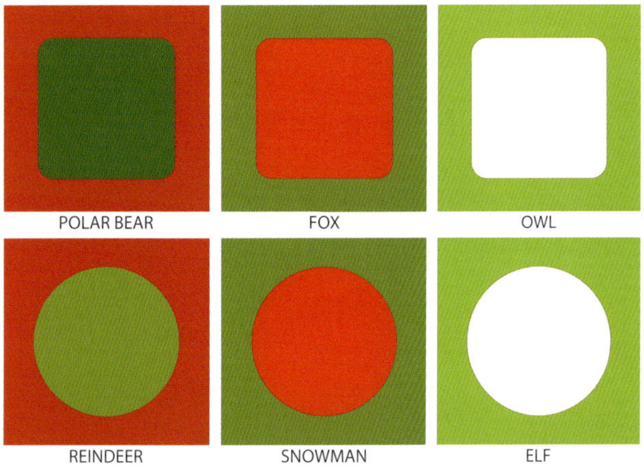

2. Lay out one 6" x 6" (15.2 x 15.2cm) piece of color felt backing for each ornament.

3. Remove the paper backing from the square and circle fabric backgrounds. Center each square or circle on the coordinating felt backing and fuse it in place.

4. Working with one ornament piece at a time, remove the paper backing, place the piece on the fabric background, and fuse it in place.

5. Using a coordinating thread, appliqué the ornament to the felt with a decorative stitch. Use a simple blanket stitch.

6. Trace the small holly leaves on freezer paper, then iron the paper onto the medium green felt. Cut the leaves and arrange them as shown.

7. Use a straight stitch to sew a line down the center of each leaf. A stylus will help keep the leaf in place as you sew. Use a hand needle and sew the red buttons between the holly leaves on each ornament.

8. Sew the eyes in place and embroider the mouth on the polar bear, fox, reindeer, and snowman using two strands of embroidery floss. Repeat with the nose and the mouth on the elf.

> **TIP**: Alternatively, you could use a thin, bleed-proof quilt marker to draw the mouths.

BACK OF ORNAMENTS

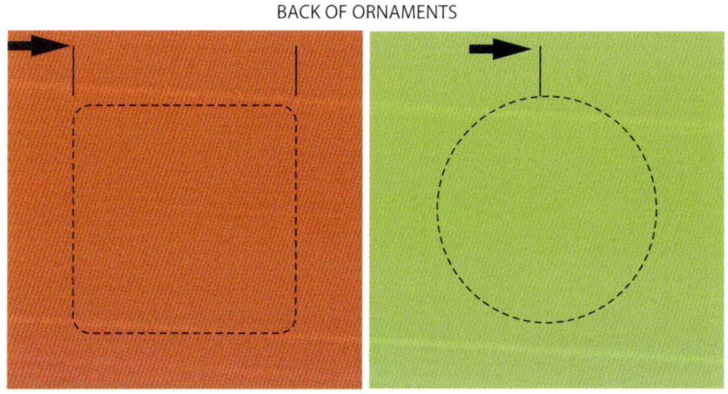

9. Mark the top edge ½" (1.2cm) in from each fabric edge on the square ornaments and find the top center on the round ones.

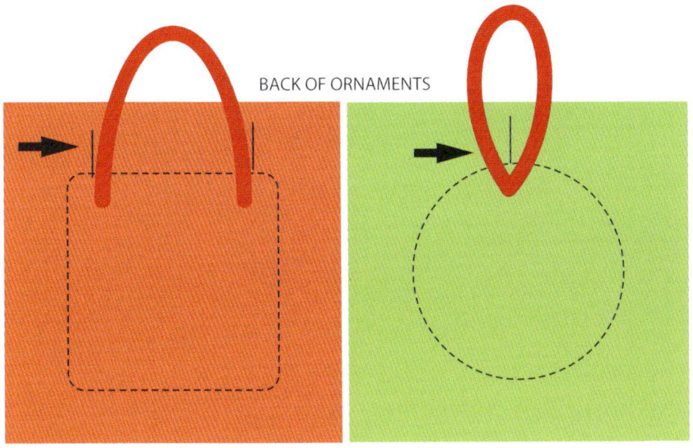

10. Place one of the 7" (17.8cm) pieces of the red grosgrain ribbon on the back of the square and round ornaments, as shown. Pin the ribbon in place from the front. Make sure the ribbon is below the stitching line on the back of the fabric to ensure it is sewn in place.

11. Take the remaining pieces of felt and place each ornament front on its coordinating back.

12. Along the edge of the fabric square or circle, begin sewing with a straight stitch and a coordinating thread, starting at the bottom right edge and working around to the bottom left edge. Leave enough space open to insert stuffing.

13. Take a small amount of stuffing and stuff each ornament until it is just full enough so you can sew the opening shut. Stuff, then sew each ornament closed.

14. Carefully trim the ornament along the edge about ⅛" (3.2mm) away from the appliqué edge. Make sure you do not cut the ribbon hanger.

15. Make a small bow with the red satin ribbon and attach one to each ornament with a small stitch (or use a hot glue gun).

Merry Banner

Made by Deb Grogan.

Let's get MERRY! While the Christmas tree is the quintessential grande dame of holiday decorating, the fireplace can also be a focal point for gatherings, storytelling, and cherished traditions. What better way to celebrate this special space than with a handmade banner that captures the spirit of the season?

The banner finishes at 32" (81.3cm) long; the flags finish at 6" x 12½" (15.2 x 31.8cm) each.

MATERIALS

- Merry Banner templates (page 66)
- 1 yard (91.4cm) lightweight fusible web of choice, usually 18" (45.7cm) wide
- 5" x 5" (12.7 x 12.7cm) piece of freezer paper, for small holly leaves
- ¼ yard (23.1cm) off-white fabric, for letters
- (5) 6" x 12" (15.2 x 30.5cm) assorted red prints, for fabric flags
- 4" x 4" (10.2 x 10.2cm) medium green felt square, for small holly leaves
- (2) 8" x 8" (20.3 x 20.3cm) assorted green prints, for holly leaves
- 27" x 36" (68.6 x 91.4cm) light green felt
- (2) 8" x 8" (20.3 x 20.3cm) medium green felt squares, for holly leaves
- (5) ¼" (6.4mm) red buttons
- Hand needle
- 1½ yards (137.2cm) red/white striped grosgrain ribbon, ⅜" (1cm) wide
- (10) 6mm bells (optional)
- 3 yards (274.3cm) red grosgrain ribbon, ⅝" (1.6cm) wide

Making the Flags

1. Trace the templates, except for the small holly leaves, onto the paper side of the fusible web. Trace the holly leaves onto the freezer paper.

2. Fuse the letters and fabric flags to the wrong side of the fabric indicated on the templates. Fuse the small holly leaves to the 5" x 5" (12.7 x 12.7cm) medium green felt. Set the felt aside.

3. Cut out each letter and fabric flag, then remove the paper backing from each piece. Place a letter on a fabric flag: center each letter and position it 4" (10.2cm) from the top of the fabric flag. Fuse the letter in place.

MERRY

4. Cut five strips 7" (17.8cm) wide from the 27" x 36" (68.6 x 91.4cm) piece of light green felt. Square up. Fold the felt in half lengthwise.

5. Remove the paper backing from the fabric flags. Place the flags on the felt strip, with the tops of the flags ½" (1.3cm) from the fold in the top of the strip.

6. Lay the felt out flat and, using a coordinating thread, appliqué the flags to the felt with a decorative stitch like a blanket stitch. Repeat for each letter.

7. Cut the small holly leaves fused to the medium green felt. Arrange them as shown. Using a quilt marker, place a dot in between the holly leaves to mark where the red button goes. Use a straight stitch to sew a line down the center of each leaf. Use a hand needle to sew on the red buttons.

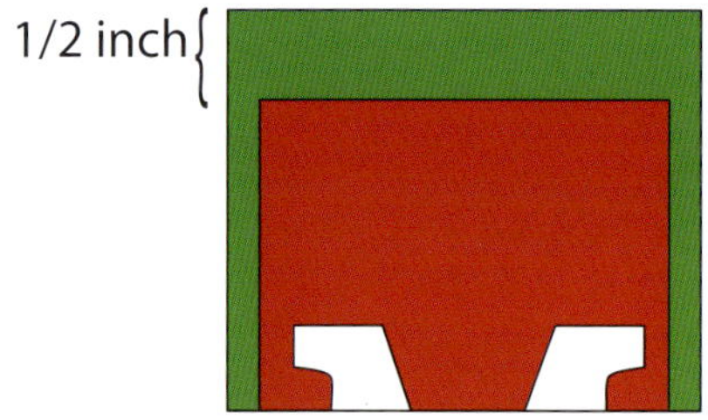

8. Fold down the top of the 7" x 27" (17.8 x 68.6cm) piece of felt so that the top of the fabric flag is ½" (1.3cm) from the fold. If it is not, readjust the fold.

9. Using a coordinating thread and bobbin, edge stitch around the edge of the flag through the folded felt.

TIP: Doubling the thickness of felt does a few things: a) adds stability, b) adds texture, c) adds a decorative touch, and d) creates a channel to thread the ribbon through for hanging. It also hides all the threads from the appliqué process!

MAKING BOWS

Does making bows challenge you, especially the small ones? Scan the QR code to watch a quick tutorial on making bows fast and easy.

scan for more information

10. With the straight edge of a ruler, trim the two sides of each letter ⅛"–¼" (3.2–6.4mm) away from the fabric flag, creating a felt "border." Use a pair of scissors to cut the *V* between the flag tails. Draw a line as a guide if needed.

11. Fuse the holly leaves to the 8" x 8" (20.3 x 20.3cm) medium green felt. Leave enough space between leaves to allow for cutting them out and creating a ⅛"–¼" (3.2–6.4mm) felt border. Appliqué the leaves to the felt with a decorative stitch. Layer over the second felt piece and straight stitch around the leaves, repeating the process you used to create the flags.

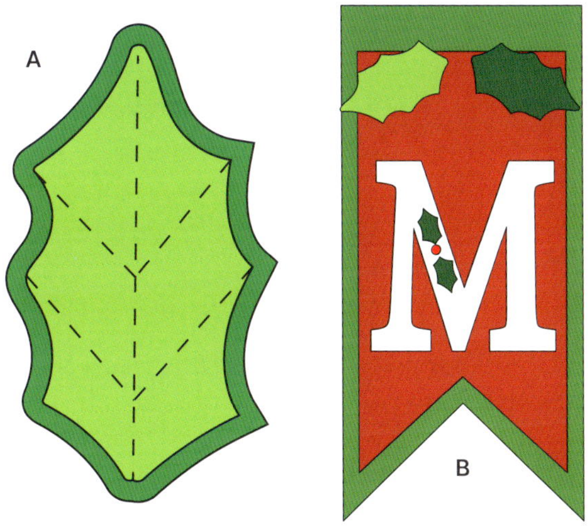

12. Using a quilt marker, draw the leaf veins and straight stitch them with a coordinating thread (**A**). Position a leaf on the top portion of each flag (**B**). Follow the center vein on each leaf and stitch the leaf in place.

13. From the red/white striped grosgrain ribbon, cut five 10" (25.4cm) pieces. Make bows for the centers of the holly leaves. Sew or hot glue the bows in place. Sew a bell to the tip of each flag point.

14. Lay out the flags in order. Find the center of the red ribbon and mark the center. Use a stylus to push the ribbon through the flag channels. They are sewn slightly smaller than the ⅝" (1.6cm) ribbon to keep the flags in place once strung. The first *R* should be positioned roughly in the center. Leave 1" (2.5cm) or so of space between each letter.

Oh Joy!

Made by Madeline Harris and Deb Grogan; quilted by Amy Lobsiger.

This wall hanging is not only a fun piece of décor, but also versatile enough to double as a table square, making it a useful addition to your holiday decorating. Welcome guests into your home with a sweet, smiling snowman, or place the quilt at the center of your dining or serving table to create a cozy, inviting atmosphere for family and friends to gather around.

All seams are sewn with a ¼" (6.4mm) seam allowance and right sides together (RST). All cuts are made using the width of fabric (WOF). Press as you go; all seams are pressed to the dark side unless otherwise indicated.

The quilt finishes at 38" x 38" (96.5 x 96.5cm).

MATERIALS

- Oh Joy! templates (pages 67–71)
- 2 yards (182.8cm) lightweight fusible web of choice, usually 18" (45.7cm) wide, for all appliqué
- **Fabric A:** ⅔ yard (61cm) white with holly print, for Border 2
- **Fabric B:** ½ yard (45.7cm) red textured tonal; for Border 1, sashing, and Border 2 cornerstones
- **Fabric C:** ⅓ yard (30.5cm) light cream textured tonal; for letters *J*, *Y*, and bottom of snowman backgrounds
- **Fabric D:** ½ yard (45.7cm) light green textured tonal; for snowflake, snowman backgrounds, Border 1 cornerstones, and large holly appliqués
- **Fabric E:** Fat Eighth (22.9 x 55.9cm) red polka dot, for letters *Y* and *J*
- **Fabric F:** Fat Eighth (22.9 x 55.9cm) dark green polka dot, for tree middle and medium holly
- **Fabric G:** Fat Eighth (22.9 x 55.9cm) medium green print; for tree bottom, small holly, and medium holly
- **Fabric H:** ⅓ yard (30.5cm) light cream tonal snowflake; for tree top, snowman, and snowflake
- **Fabric I:** 10" x 10" (25.4 x 25.4cm) brown solid, for tree trunk and snowman arm
- **Fabric J:** 5" x 5" (12.7 x 12.7cm) deep yellow textural, for star
- **Fabric K:** Fat Eighth (22.9 x 55.9cm) black print, for snowman hat
- **Fabric L:** Fat Eighth (22.9 x 55.9cm) red print, for hat band and scarf
- **Fabric M:** 5" x 5" (12.7 x 12.7cm) pink solid, for snowman cheeks
- **Fabric N:** 5" x 5" (12.7 x 12.7cm) orange solid, for snowman nose
- Matching thread, for seams and appliqué
- 2⅝ yards (238.6cm) backing fabric of your choice, 44" (111.8cm) wide
- **Binding:** ¼ yard (22.9cm) green textural
  - We prefer a 2" (5.1cm) cut, but if you prefer a 2½" (6.4cm) cut, use ⅓ yard (30.5cm) green textural
- Tearaway stabilizer, as needed (optional)

BUTTONS

- (6) ⅝" (1.6cm) red, for holly berries on letters *J* and *Y*
- (5) 3⁄16" (4.8mm) black, for mouth on snowman
- (3) ⅜" (1cm) red, for holly berries on hat
- (2) 1½" (3.8cm) red; for holly berries, border, cornerstones
- (2) 1¼" (3.2cm) red; for holly berries, border, cornerstones
- (2) 1" (2.5cm) red; for holly berries, border, cornerstones
- (2) ½" (1.2cm) black, for snowman chest
- (2) ¼" (6.4mm) black, for eyes on snowman

Cutting Instructions

I recommend always cutting the fabric strips before you cut out the appliqués.

FABRIC A

- (4) 5½" (14cm) x WOF strips, subcut:
  - (4) 5½" x 28½" (14 x 72.4cm) strips, for Border 2

FABRIC B

- (5) 1½" (3.8cm) x WOF strips, subcut:
  - (5) 1½" x 26½" (3.8 x 67.3cm) strips
- (2) 1½" x 12½" (3.8 x 31.8cm) strips, for sashing and Border 1
- (1) 5½" (14cm) x WOF strip, subcut:
  - (4) 5½" x 5½" (14 x 14cm) squares, for Border 2 cornerstones

FABRIC C

- (1) 8½" (21.6cm) x WOF strips, subcut:
  - (2) 8½" x 12½" (21.6 x 31.8cm) rectangles
- (1) 6½" x 13½" (16.5 x 34.3cm) rectangle, for letters *J* and *Y* background and snowman blocks

FABRIC D

- (1) 13½" x 20½" (34.3 x 52.1cm) rectangle
- (1) 8½" (21.6cm) x WOF strip, subcut:
  - (1) 8½" x 20½" (21.6 x 52.1cm) rectangle
- (1) 8½" x 12½" (21.6 x 31.8cm) rectangle
  - Use the remainder of this strip for the large holly appliqués
- (1) 1½" (3.8cm) x WOF strip, subcut:
  - (4) 1½" x 1½" (3.8 x 3.8cm) squares, for Border 1 cornerstones

BINDING

- (4) 2" (5.1cm) OR (4) 2½" (6.4cm) strips, based on your preference

Making the Appliqué Pieces

1. Fabrics E through N are all used for appliqué. Trace, fuse, and cut out all the appliqué pieces. Do not remove the paper backing until you are ready to place the pieces. Refer to appliqué basics instructions on pages 14–16 as needed.

2. Lay out the two 8½" x 12½" (21.6 x 31.8cm) Fabric C rectangles and one Fabric D as shown. Find the center of the top block and mark it with a quilt marker or pencil. This will be your guide to placing the letters and snowflake.

3. Remove the paper backing (do so for each appliqué piece as you go) from letters *J*, *Y*, and the snowflake. Place the pieces on the background rectangles. Center the letters without the holly. Once you are happy with their placement, fuse the pieces in place.

4. Place three Fabric F and three Fabric G medium holly leaves as shown. Fuse them in place. **Note:** You can appliqué these blocks now if you choose to. Smaller blocks are easier to manage. Or you can wait until the entire quilt center is sewn together, and then do the appliqué.

5. Sew together 6½" x 13½" (16.5 x 34.3cm) Fabric C rectangle and the 13½" x 20½" (34.3 x 52.1cm) Fabric D rectangle on the 13½" (16.5cm) ends.

6. Place the arm and scarf (shown in gray) but do not fuse them in place. Using the Visual Guide (page 32), place snowman and tree appliqué pieces in number order. Tuck the pieces under the overlapping pieces so no raw edges of fabric will show. Align the left edge and the bottom of the snowman with the edges of the background block. They will not be appliquéd but sewn into the seam.

7. Once you are happy with the placement, remove the arm and scarf first. They will be appliquéd after the quilt center is sewn. Fuse the rest of the pieces in place.

8. Using a coordinating thread, appliqué the letters *J* and *Y* and the snowflake (if you have not already), followed by the snowman and tree.

TEMPLATE DOWNLOAD

Scan the QR code and download a full-size version of the layout guide for the snowman and tree block. You will need to print it on letter size paper and piece it together following the instructions.

scan for more information

Visual Guide

Assembling the Wall Hanging

9. Lay out the letter blocks, snowflake block, and two 1½" x 12½" (3.8 x 31.8cm) Fabric B strips. Sew them together.

10. Sew a 1½" x 26½" (3.8 x 67.3cm) Fabric B strip to the left side of the snowman tree block.

11. Sew the left side of the quilt (letters and snowflake) to the snowman tree block.

12. Place the snowman scarf and arm, and fuse them in place. You may appliqué these pieces now, or wait until you have sewn on the borders and placed and fused the large holly leaves in the corners.

BORDERS

13. With the four remaining 1½" x 26½" (3.8 x 67.3cm) Fabric B strips, sew one to each side of the quilt center. Sew one 1½" x 1½" (3.8 x 3.8cm) Fabric D square to each end of the last two. Sew one to the top and one to the bottom as shown.

14. With the four 5½" x 28½" (14 x 72.4cm) Fabric A strips, sew one to the right side and one to the left side of the quilt. Sew a 5½" x 5½" (14 x 14cm) Fabric B square to each end of the remaining two strips, then sew one to the top and one to the bottom of the quilt.

15. Place a large holly appliqué on the upper-left corner and one on the lower-right corner of the quilt. If you have not appliquéd the arm and scarf of the snowman yet, do that now, along with the holly leaves.

Finishing

16. Layer the quilt top, batting, and backing. Either hand or machine quilt as desired. If you are using quilting services, leave enough extra on all sides of the batting and backing for your longarmer. Check with them to see what they request for overage.

17. Apply the buttons to the snowman and between the holly leaves as shown.

18. Sew the binding strips together, end to end and at a 45-degree angle. Bind as desired.

OPTIONAL HANGING SLEEVE

Cut a 5" x 37" (12.7 x 94cm) strip of fabric. Fold each end in ¼" (6.4mm) twice, and sew along the edge. Fold the strip in half with the wrong sides together, and place the strip along the top of the quilt before you attach the binding. Center the sleeve, pin it in place, and continue adding the binding.

Peppermint and Holly

Made by Madeline Harris and Deb Grogan; quilted by Amy Lobsiger.

Celebrate the season with the Peppermint and Holly table runner and placemats. Swirling down the center, peppermint pinwheel candies are intertwined with lush holly leaves and red holly berries as well as sprays of pine, adding a whimsical yet elegant charm to your table. The simple piecing and appliqué work make this striking but easy-to-make set a joyful addition to any holiday season table.

Some practical tips: Before you begin, please read through all instructions. All seams are sewn with a ¼" (6.4mm) seam allowance and RST (right sides together). All cuts are made using the WOF (width of fabric). Press as you go.

- The table runner finishes at 20" x 60" (50.8 x 152.4cm).
- The two placemats finish at 12" x 20" (30.5 x 50.8cm) each.
- The dish towel finishes at 16" x 28" (40.6 x 71.1cm).

TOOLS & MATERIALS

- Peppermint and Holly templates (pages 72–73)
- **Fabric A:** 1½ yards (152.4cm) white textured tonal; for block, Border 2, appliqué center, peppermints, and holly berries on towel
- **Fabric B:** ¼ yard (22.9cm) small red polka dot, for peppermints
- **Fabric C:** ½ yard (45.7cm) large red polka dot, for block and Border 2 cornerstones
- **Fabric D:** 12" (30.5cm) red and white stripe, for sashing and Border 1
- **Fabric E:** ⅞–1 yard (80–91.4cm) dark green small print, for binding, Border 1 cornerstones, holly leaf, and vine appliqué
    - Included: optional extra yardage for 2½" (6.4cm) binding (we use 2" [5.1cm])
- **Fabric F:** ⅛ yard (11.4cm) each of light green, medium-light green, and medium green prints; for holly leaves
- **Fabric G:** 8" x 8" (20.3 x 20.3cm) red solid, for holly berries
- **Fabric H:** ⅛ yard (11.4cm) light green texture, for pine spray appliqués
- 2 yards (182.8cm) lightweight fusible web of choice, usually 18" wide (45.7cm), for all appliqué
- 16" x 30" (40.6 x 76.2cm) toweling by the yard (or pre-hemmed dish towel)
- Matching thread for seams and appliqué
- 2 yards (182.8cm) backing fabric of your choice, 44" (111.8cm) wide
    - Amount will easily fit the runner and two placemats on the same backing, with at least 4" (10.2cm) overage each side for quilting
- 2 yards (182.8cm) batting, 44" (11.8cm) wide (or packaged twin size)

Cutting Instructions

FABRIC A

- (1) 12½" (31.8cm) x WOF strip, subcut:
  - (1) 12½" x 25½" (31.8 x 64.8cm) rectangles, for runner appliqué center
  - (4) 3½" x 12½ (8.9 x 31.8cm) end sections, for placemats
- (1) 8" (20.3cm) x WOF strip, subcut:
  - (4) 8" x 8" (20.3 x 20.3cm) squares, for block HSTs
- (1) 6½" (16.5cm) x WOF strip, subcut:
  - (4) 6½" x 6½" (16.5 x 16.5cm) squares, for block center
- (5) 3½" (8.9cm) x WOF strips, subcut:
  - (2) 3½" x 40½" (8.9 x 102.9cm) strips, for runner Border 2
  - (2) 3½" x 14½" (8.9 x 31cm) strips, for runner Border 2
  - (2) 3½" x 13½" (8.9 x 34.3cm) strips, for runner Border 2
  - (16) 3½" x 3½" (8.9 x 8.9cm) squares, for block
- (1) 5" (12.7cm) x WOF strip, subcut:
  - (10) 5" x 5" (12.7 x 12.7cm) squares, peppermints HSTs
  - Use remaining scrap for towel mistletoe berry appliqués

FABRIC B

- (1) 5" (12.7cm) x WOF strip, subcut:
  - (10) 5" x 5" (12.7 x 12.7cm) squares, for peppermints HSTs

FABRIC C

- (1) 8" (20.3cm) x WOF strip, subcut:
  - (4) 8" x 8" (20.3 x 20.3cm) squares, block HSTs
- (1) 3½" (8.9cm) x WOF strip, subcut:
  - (4) 3½" x 3½" (8.9 x 8.9cm) squares, for Border 2 cornerstones

FABRIC D

- (6) 1½" (3.8cm) x WOF strips, subcut:
  - (16) 1½" x 12½" (3.8 x 31.8cm) strips, for sashing and Border 1

FABRIC E

- (9) 2" (5.1cm) x WOF strips, for binding
  - If using a wider binding, cut (9) 2½" (6.4cm) x WOF strips
- (1) 1½" (3.8cm) x WOF strip, subcut:
  - (10) 1½" x 1½" (3.8 x 3.8cm) strips, for Border 1 cornerstones
  - Use the remainder for vines and holly appliqués

Making the Appliqué Pieces

1. Fabrics F through H are all used for appliqué. Trace, fuse, and cut out all the appliqué pieces. For the 42 holly leaves in Fabric F, distribute the templates between the three fabrics, then mix up the different sizes to add texture and variety to the pieces. Do not remove the paper backing until you are ready to place the pieces. Refer to appliqué basics instructions on pages 14–16 as needed.

Making the Star Blocks

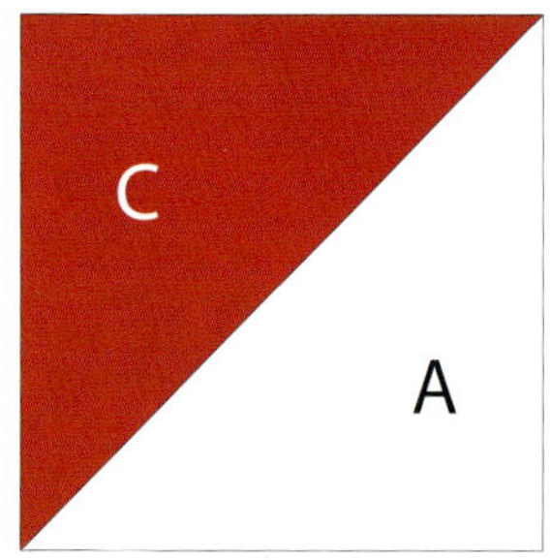

2. Refer to Half-Square Triangles (page 17) to make 32 total HST units with 8" x 8" (20.3 x 20.3cm) Fabric A and C squares. Press open and trim to 3½" x 3½" (8.9 x 8.9cm).

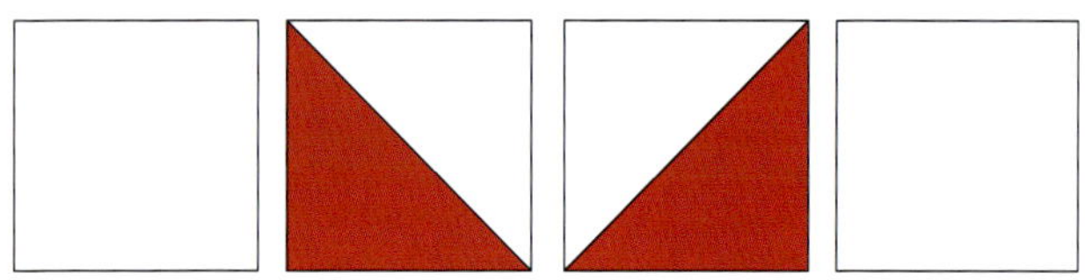

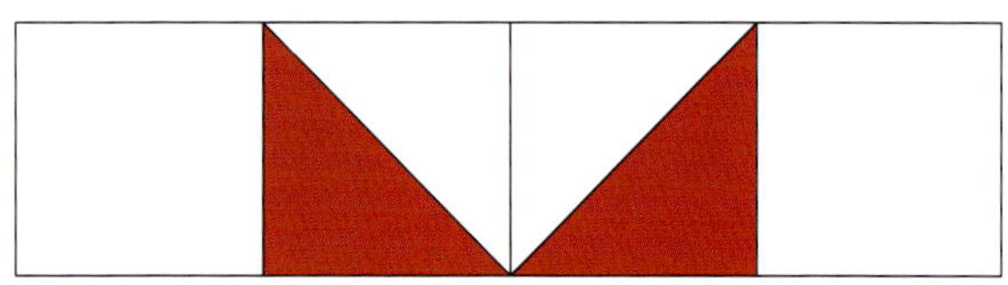

3. Lay out a 3½" x 3½" (8.9 x 8.9cm) Fabric A square, two HSTs, and another 3½" (8.9cm) Fabric A square. Pay attention to the orientation of the HST units. Sew them together to make Row 1. Repeat to make Row 3.

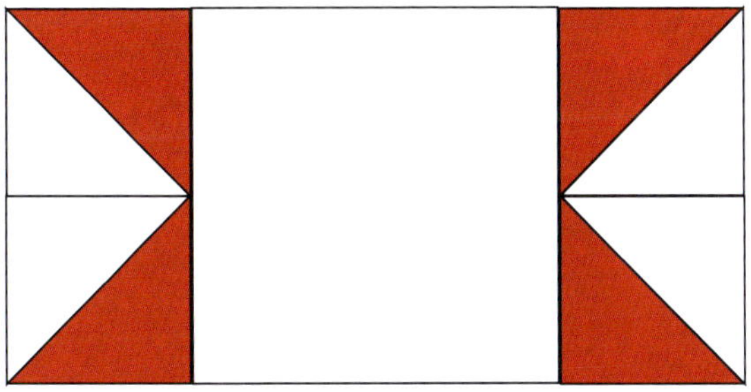

4. Sew two HSTs together, then another pair. Sew to the left and right of a 6½" x 6½" (16.5 x 16.5cm) Fabric A square to make Row 2.

5. Join Rows 1 through 3 as shown. This makes one Star Block, measuring 12½" x 12½" (31.8 x 31.8cm) unfinished.

6. Repeat to make four blocks total. You will use two for the runner and one for each placemat.

Making the Peppermint Candies

7. Make 80 total HSTs with 5" x 5" (12.7 x 12.7cm) Fabric A and B squares. Press the seams open to reduce bulk.

> **TIP**: You do not need to trim these HSTs, and they do not need to be perfect. It's important to make sure you match points and seams, but the overall size after sewing does not matter, as they will be cut into circles.

8. Lay out four of the HST units as shown. Sew together to create a Pinwheel Block. Repeat to make 20 total, roughly 3½"–4" (8.9–10.2cm). Press all seams open.

9. If you have not already traced, fused, and cut out all the appliqué pieces, do so now.

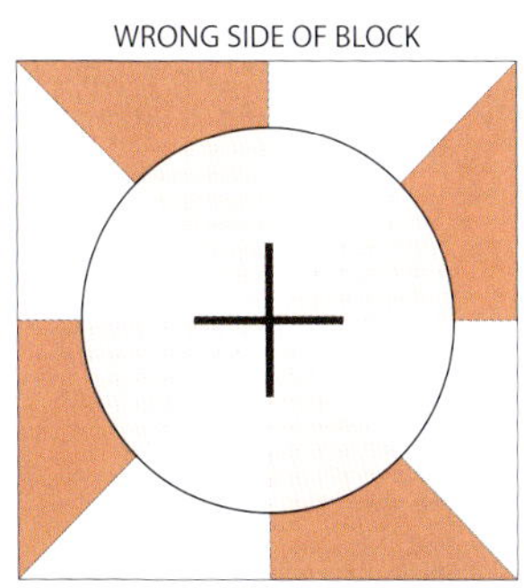

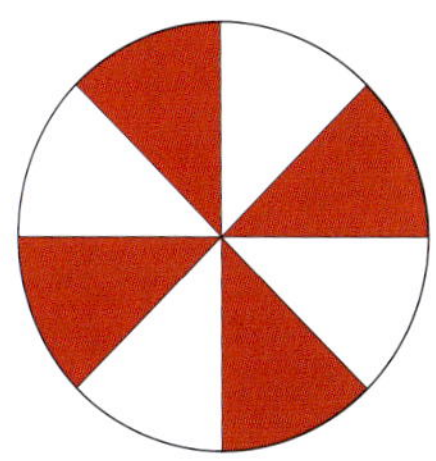

10. Lay a Pinwheel Block right side down on a light source. Place the traced circle of fusible over the block with the bullseye on the center seams. Fuse. Make sure all the seams are open. Repeat for six large and 14 small peppermints.

Making the Runner and Placemats

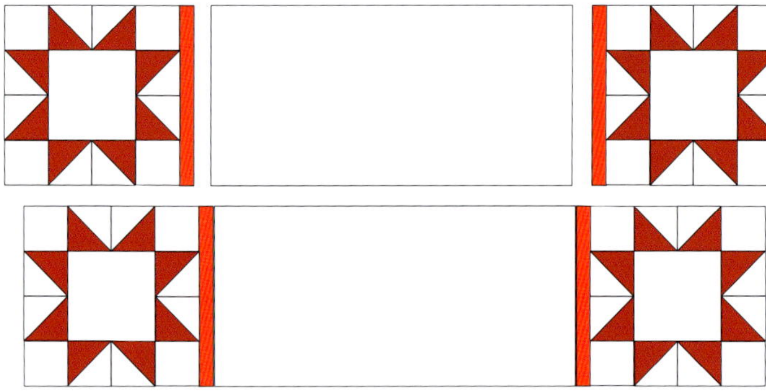

11. Sew a 1½" x 12½" (3.8 x 31.8cm) Fabric D sashing strip to one side of a Star Block. Repeat. Sew together the blocks and the 12½" x 25½" (31.8 x 64.8cm) Fabric A piece.

12. Sew a 1½" x 12½" (3.8 x 31.8cm) Fabric D sashing strip to each side of a Star Block. Repeat. Sew a 3½" x 12½" (8.9 x 31.8cm) Fabric A piece to each end, then repeat with the second block.

PLACING THE APPLIQUÉ PIECES

13. Remove the paper backing and lay out the appliqué pieces. Appliqué pieces in place on the runner and placemats using a coordinating thread and decorative stitch of your choice. Use a stabilizer if needed.

LAYOUT GUIDE

You can lay out the appliqués visually or you can download a printable, full-size layout guide for the runner and placemat by following the QR code.

scan for more information

Your kitchen deserves some festive flair! This dish towel is easy to make and makes a huge impact.

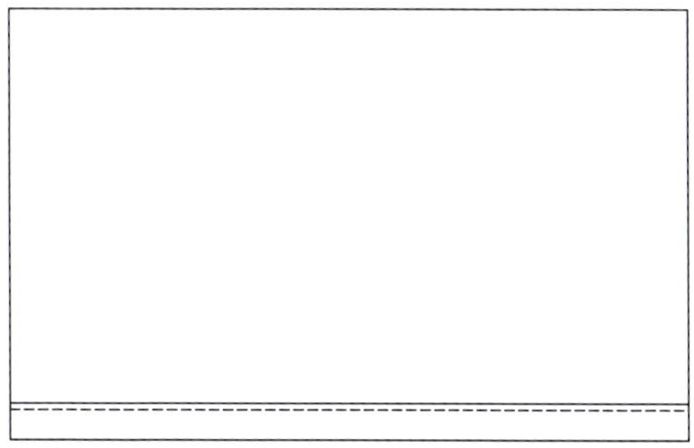

TIP: Press, but do not move the iron back and forth, as the towel is a looser weave and may become distorted.

14. If you are using a pre-hemmed towel, skip to step 16. If you opted for toweling by the yard, lay the toweling on the ironing table, then lift and place the iron along the edges. Let the toweling cool before moving it and the edges will stay flat.

15. Fold up the bottom unfinished edge of the toweling ½" (1.2cm) toward the wrong side, fold again, and press. Repeat for the other end. Sew along the folded edge using matching top and bobbin thread.

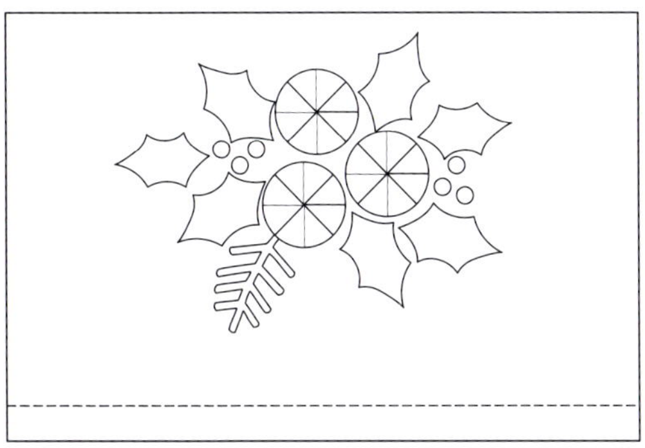

16. Appliqué the pieces to finish the towel.

Assembling the Runner

BORDER 1

17. Sew a 1½" x 40½" (3.8 x 102.9cm) Fabric D sashing strip to each end of the runner.

18. Sew a 1½" x 1½" (3.8 x 3.8cm) Fabric E square to the end of a 1½" x 40½" (3.8 x 102.9cm) Fabric D sashing strip. Continue for four total sashing strips with cornerstones in between and one on each end. Repeat for a second sashing border.

19. Sew one sashing border to the top of the runner and one to the bottom.

LONGARMING CONSIDERATIONS

For the quilting on my runner and placemats, I asked my longarmer to use a very pale pink thread. This choice was intended to slightly lift the quilting in the negative space without too much emphasis on the red fabrics. The result was stunning, and the holly and berry vine pattern complemented the overall design perfectly. I love Amy's ability to truly "read" quilts and intuitively know what they need. When selecting thread colors and quilting designs, especially with appliqué, it's essential to choose quilting designs that enhance your work without overwhelming it. The combination of design and thread color brings just the right balance of texture and detail to these projects.

BORDER 2

20. Sew together a 3½" x 40½" (8.9 x 102.9cm) and 3½" x 13½" (8.9 x 34.9cm) Fabric A piece for a 53½" (135.9cm) border. Repeat for another border piece. Sew one to the top of the runner and one to the bottom.

21. Sew a 3½" x 3½" (8.9 x 8.9cm) Fabric C square to each end of a 3½" x 14½" (3.9 x 36.8cm) Fabric A piece. Repeat. Sew one unit to each end of the runner.

Finishing

22. Layer the tops, batting, and backing. Either hand or machine quilt as desired. If you are using quilting services, leave enough extra on all sides of your batting and backing for your longarmer. Check with them to see what they request for overage.

23. Sew the binding strips together, end to end at a 45-degree angle. Bind as desired.

Home for the Holidays

Made by Madeline Harris and Deb Grogan; quilted by Amy Lobsiger.

There's nothing more relaxing than cuddling up with a cozy quilt in front of the fireplace after a long day or a holiday meal. This quilt, done in red, green, and cream, captures the spirit of the holiday season. A simple block design gives the illusion of pine trees, while appliquéd Christmas berries add a touch of holiday whimsy. Paired with a matching toss pillow, this duo transforms your living room into a warm and inviting holiday retreat.

Before you begin, please read through all instructions. All seams are sewn with a ¼" (6.4mm) seam allowance and RST (right sides together). All cuts are made using the WOF (width of fabric). Press as you go. The yardage for the quilt does not change if you do not make the pillow; the extra blocks for the pillow are created with yardage left over from the quilt. The pillow back will be made using two pieces of fabric to create an "envelope" to add pillow inserts and remove for washing.

TIP: Trade your Christmas berries for fall leaves and use earth tones and fall colors to create a fall set. Or use light or bright colors and appliqué flowers for a spring or summer theme.

- **The quilt finishes at 58" x 70" (147.3 x 177.8cm).**
- **The pillow finishes at 24" x 24" (61 x 61cm).**

TOOLS & MATERIALS

- Home for the Holidays templates (page 78)
- 2 yards (182.8cm) lightweight fusible web of choice, usually 18" (45.7cm) wide, for all appliqué
- **Fabric A**: 1⅔ yards (152.4cm) red textured tonal, for Blocks 1 and 2 cornerstones
- **Fabric B**: ⅔ yard (61cm) green textured tonal, for Block 1
- **Fabric C**: 3 yards (274.3cm) light cream tonal snowflake; for Block 1, Block 2, and border
- **Fabric D**: Fat Eighth (22.9 x 55.9cm) light green textured tonal, for small leaf
- **Fabric E**: ¼ yard (11.4cm) medium green print, for large and small leaf
- **Fabric F**: ⅓ yard (30.5cm) red polka dot, for Christmas berries
- **Fabric G**: 1⅓ yards (122cm) red solid, for binding and pillow back
- Matching thread for seams and appliqué
- 4¼ yards (388.6cm) backing fabric of your choice, 44" (111.8cm) wide; for quilt
- 18" (45.7cm) binding, for quilt
- 1 yard (91.4cm) backing or use a scrap at least 30" x 30" (76.2 x 76.2cm) square, for pillow front
- 1 yard (91.4cm) batting, for pillow front
- Black embroidery floss, for berry stigmas
- Embroidery hand needle
- 26" x 26" (66 x 66cm) pillow insert

Cutting Instructions

Cut the fabric strips before you cut out the appliqué pieces.

FABRIC A

- (2) 10" (25.4cm) x WOF strips, subcut:
  - (8) 10" x 10" (25.4 x 25.4cm) squares, for Block 1 (if not making the pillow, subcut 7)
- (2) 13" (33cm) x WOF strips, subcut:
  - (6) 13" x 13" (33 x 33cm) squares, for Block 2 (if not making the pillow, subcut 5)
- (1) 5½" (14cm) x WOF strip, subcut:
  - (4) 5½" x 5½" (14 x 14 cm) squares, for border cornerstones

FABRIC B

- (2) 10" (25.4cm) x WOF strips, subcut:
  - (6) 10" x 10" (25.4 x 25.4cm) squares, for Block 1 (if not making the pillow, subcut 5)

FABRIC C

- (4) 10" (25.4cm) x WOF strips, subcut:
  - (14) 10" x 10" (25.4 x 25.4cm) squares, for Block 1 (if not making the pillow, subcut 12)
- (2) 13" (33cm) x WOF strips, subcut:
  - (6) 13" x 13" (33 x 33cm) squares, for Block 2 (if not making the pillow, subcut 5)
- (1) 5½" (14cm) x WOF strip, subcut:
  - (4) 5½" x 5½" (14 x 14 cm) squares, for border cornerstones

FABRIC G

- (7) 2" (5.1cm) x WOF strips, for binding
  - If using a wider binding, cut (7) 2½" (6.4cm) x WOF strips
- (1) 18½" (47cm) x WOF strip, subcut:
  - (2) 18½" x 12½" (47 x 31.8cm) rectangles, pillow back

Block 1

Block 1 consists of 9 HST units—5 red and cream, and 4 green and cream. You will make them using the Magic 8 Method, in which you are able to sew, cut, and make eight HST units at one time.

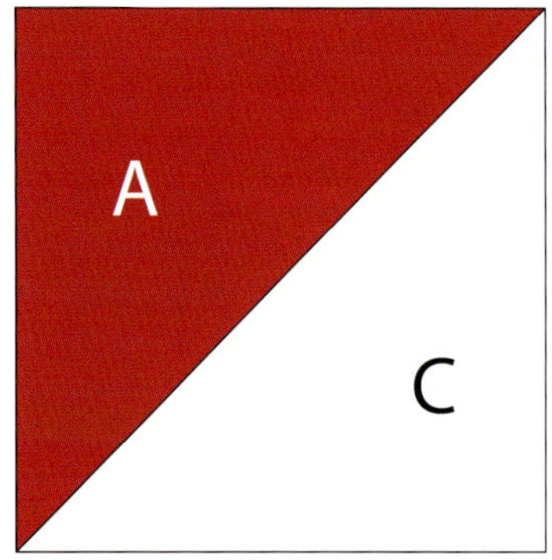

1. Refer to Half-Square Triangles (page 17) to make 58 total HST units with 10" x 10" (25.4 x 25.4cm) Fabric A and C squares. Press open and trim to 4½" x 4½" (11.4 x 11.4cm). You will have extra, as you only need 50 for the quilt.

TIP: Finger-press the HST units open first because they are cut on a bias and can become skewed. Do not use a back-and-forth ironing motion.

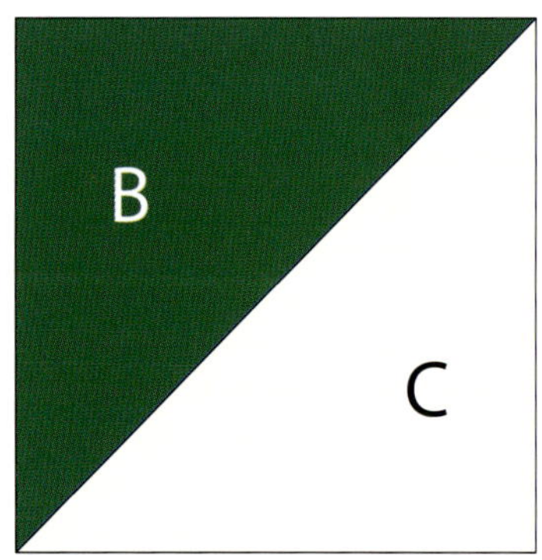

2. Make 48 total HSTs with 10" x 10" (25.4 x 25.4cm) Fabric B and C squares. Press open and trim to 4½" x 4½" (11.4 x 11.4cm). You will have extra, as you only need 40 for the quilt.

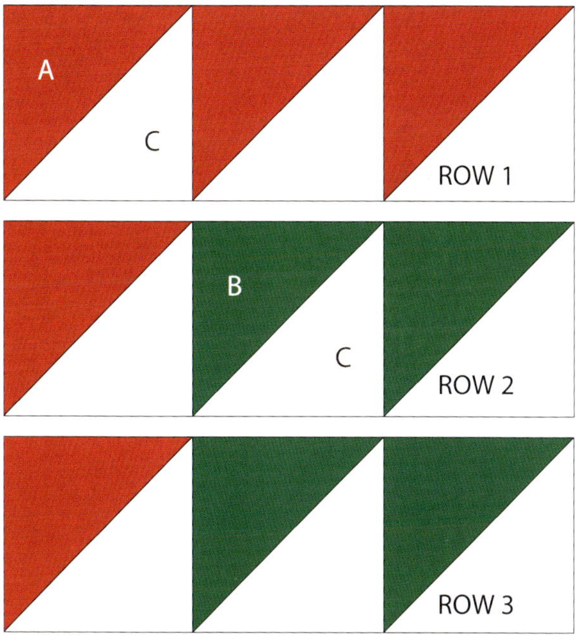

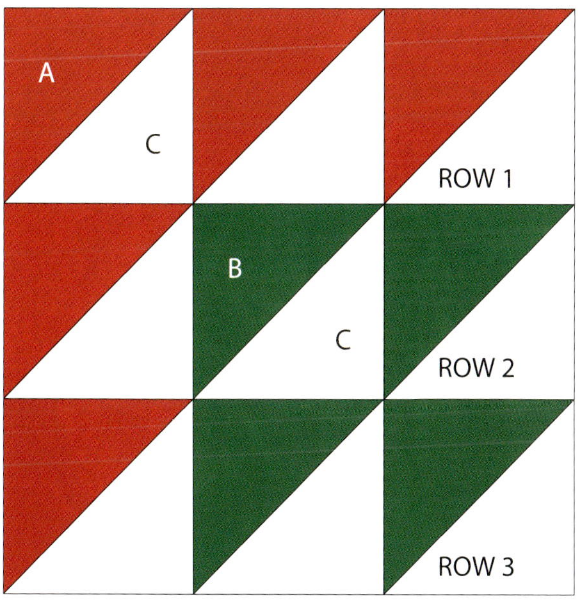

3. Lay out the HST units as shown. Sew Row 1 together, then Row 2, and finally Row 3. Sew the rows together.

4. Repeat to create 12 blocks (10 for the quilt only), measuring 12½" x 12½" (31.8 x 31.8cm) unfinished.

Block 2

There is more than one way to make HSTs. This time, we will be making the larger block two at a time instead of eight at a time.

5. Gather the six (five if making quilt only) 13" x 13" (33 x 33cm) Fabric A and C squares. Draw a line from one corner to the other on the diagonal.

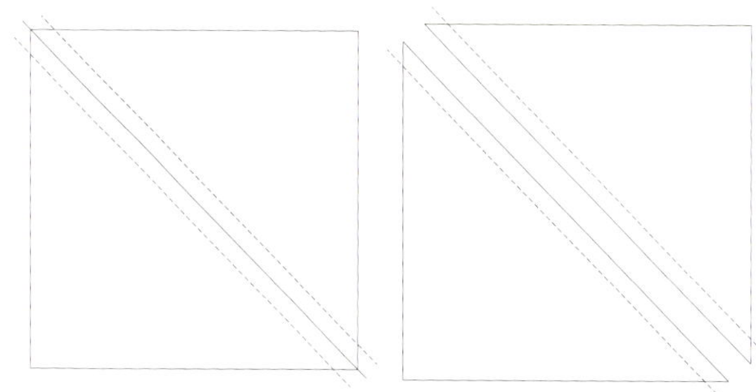

6. Sew a seam ¼" (6.4mm) to the left of the drawn line, then ¼" (6.4mm) to the right. Press then cut in half on the drawn line.

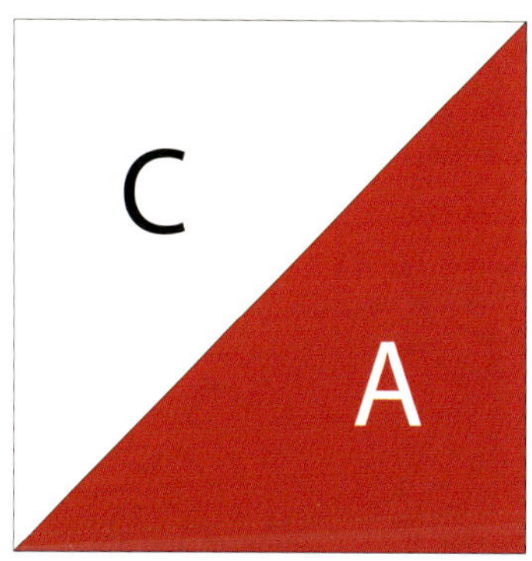

7. Press open and trim to 12½" x 12½" (31.8 x 31.8cm).

Making the Appliqué Pieces

8. If you have not already, trace, fuse, and cut out all the Christmas berry appliqué pieces. Do not remove the paper backing until you are ready to place the pieces.

9. Trace the layout guide on page 78 on a piece of paper, or lay the fabric directly on the guide page. Align the top-left corner of the block on the dotted line. This is the seam allowance. Place the appliqué pieces on the block and fuse them in place.

10. Appliqué the berries and leaves using a coordinating thread and stitch of your choice. If this quilt will be washed frequently, keep that in mind. You may want to do a satin stitch.

TIP: I have several quilts that I bring out for the holidays that do not get washed, as they get little use. Most of the time, they are draped over a piece of furniture or the quilt ladder to create more decoration. They are thrown in the dryer with a fabric sheet, fluffed, then folded and stored in a dust-free bag until the next year. I spot clean them if needed.

11. Using three to four strands of black embroidery floss, make four or five French knots close together to create the stigma. Alternately, you could sew very small black buttons in place after it is quilted.

12. Lay out 10 of Block 1 and 10 of Block 2 as shown in the Quilt Diagram. Sew each row, then sew the rows together. Set the remaining four blocks aside for the pillow.

The round holly berries break up the geometric pattern of the quilt nicely. Keep that in mind if you make a variation of this design.

Quilt Diagram

Assembling the Quilt

MAKING THE BORDER

13. Sew together a 5½" x 40½" (14 x 102.9cm) Fabric C strip and 5½" x 20½" (14 x 52.1cm) Fabric C strip to make a 60½" (153.7cm) border strip. Repeat for a second border strip. Sew one to the right side and one to the left side of the quilt.

14. Sew together a 5½" x 40½" (14 x 102.9cm) Fabric C strip and a 5½" x 8½" (14 x 21.6cm) Fabric C strip to make a 48½" (123.2cm) border strip. Sew a 5½" x 5½" (14 x 14cm) Fabric A square to each end of the strip. Repeat to make a second border strip with cornerstones. Sew one to the top and one to the bottom of the quilt.

FINISHING

15. Layer the quilt top, batting, and backing. Either hand or machine quilt as desired. If you are using quilting services, leave enough extra on all sides of your batting and backing for your longarmer. Check with them to see what they request for overage.

16. Sew the binding strips together, end to end and at a 45-degree angle. Bind as desired.

Making the Pillow

17. Lay out two of Block 1 and two of Block 2 as shown. Sew them together.

18. If you chose to quilt your pillow front, layer the front, batting, and a backing. Quilt as desired. You may need to adjust the size of your pillow back if there is any shrinkage caused by the quilting process.

19. On the 18½" (47cm) side of 18½" x 12½" (47 x 31.8cm) Fabric G rectangle, fold over one edge ½" (1.3cm) toward the wrong side and press. Fold over one more time and press again. Sew carefully along the side of the folded fabric about ⅛" (3.2mm) away from the edge. Repeat with a second Fabric G piece.

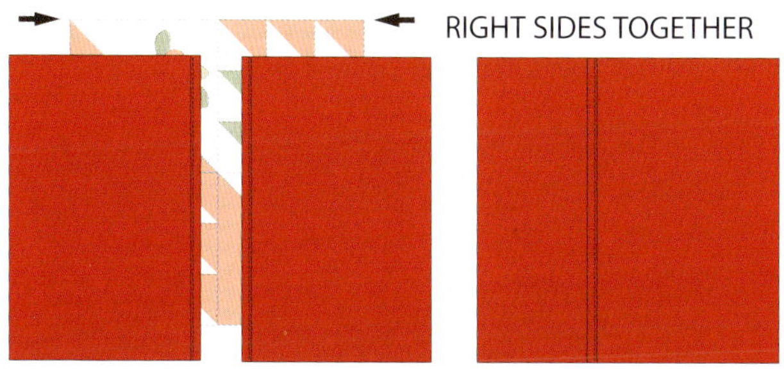

20. Line up the raw edges of each pillow back piece on the pillow front RST. There will be about 6" (15.2cm) overlap. Carefully pin the pieces in place and sew around the entire edge. Trim the excess batting and backing.

21. Turn right side out and insert the pillow form.

TIP: Make this project into a table square by adding borders to enlarge it to the size you want. If you sew them end to end and add a border, it makes a table runner. Or you can make four small pillows!

To All a Good Night

Made by Madeline Harris and Deb Grogan; quilted by Amy Lobsiger.

After a day filled with laughter, holiday cheer, and celebration, there's nothing more tempting than settling down in a cozy bed. This quilted Christmas bed runner, pieced in traditional reds, greens, and creams, paired with appliqué pillows that read "Silent Night" and "All is Calm," invite you to drift off into sweet dreams. Whether it's the glow of Christmas lights or the quiet after a bustling day, it's the perfect setting for a restful night's sleep during the busy holiday season.

All seams are sewn with a ¼" (6.4mm) seam allowance and RST (right sides together). All cuts are made using the WOF (width of fabric). Press as you go. The pillow back will be made using two pieces of fabric to create an "envelope" to add the pillow inserts and remove for washing.

Before you chose which size to make for the bed runner, consider the drop you will have depending on your mattress size and depth. Most mattresses today have thick pillow tops, making some 20" (50.8cm) high. The bed runner in the photograph is king size and fits just right.

The king bed runner finishes at 25" x 100" (63.5 x 254cm); queen, 25" x 85" (63.5 x 215.9cm); and full/twin, 25" x 70" (63.5 x 177.8cm).

The pillows finish at 12" x 20" (30.5 x 50.8cm) and 18" x 18" (45.7 x 45.7cm).

TOOLS & MATERIALS

- To All a Good Night templates (pages 74–77)
- **Fabric A:** red textural; for Border 2, Block 1 and 2, and Border 1 cornerstones
  - King: 1⅓ yards (122cm)
  - Queen: 1⅛ yards (102.9cm)
  - Full/Twin: 1 yard (91.4cm)
- **Fabric B:** cream textural; for Border 1, Border 2 cornerstones, Block 1 and 2, and pillow appliqué
  - King: 1¼ yards (114.3cm)
  - Queen: 1¼ yards (114.3cm)
  - Full/Twin: 1⅛ yards (102.9cm)
- **Fabric C:** medium green textural; for Border 2 cornerstones, Block 1 and 2, and pillow appliqué
  - King: ⅔ yard (61cm)
  - Queen: ⅔ yard (61cm)
  - Full/Twin: ½ yard (45.7cm)
- **Fabric D:** small red print; for Block 1 and 2, and rectangle pillow
  - King: ½ yard (45.7cm)
  - Queen: ½ yard (45.7cm)
  - Full/Twin: ½ yard (45.7cm)
  - Pillow: ⅔ yard (61cm)
- **Fabric E:** small dark green print; for Block 1 and 2, square pillow, and pillow appliqué
  - King: ¼ yard (22.9cm)
  - Queen: ⅛ yard (11.4cm)
  - Full/Twin: ⅛ yard (11.4cm)
  - Pillow: 1⅛ yards (102.9cm)
- **Fabric F:** dark green textural, for binding
  - King: ½ yard (45.7cm)
  - Queen: ½ yard (45.7cm)
  - Full/Twin: ⅜ yard (34.3cm)
- 1 yard (91.4cm) fusible web, for appliqué
- 12" x 20" (30.5 x 50.8cm) pillow insert
- 18" x 18" (45.7 x 45.7cm) pillow insert

Silent
Night
All
is
Calm

Cutting Instructions

Note: The king size uses three of each block, queen size uses three Block 1 and two Block 2, and full/twin size uses two of each block.

	King	Queen	Full/Twin
Fabric A	(5) 4½" (11.4cm) x WOF strips, subcut:	(5) 4½" (11.4cm) x WOF strips, subcut:	(4) 4½" (11.4cm) x WOF strips, subcut:
	(4) 4½" x 40½" (11.4 x 102.9cm) strips	(2) 4½" x 40½" (11.4 x 102.9cm) strips	(2) 4½" x 40½" (11.4 x 102.9cm) strips
	(2) 4½" x 17½" (11.4 x 44.5cm) rectangles	(2) 4½" x 37½" (11.4 x 92.3cm) strips	(2) 4½" x 17½" (11.4 x 44.5cm) rectangles
	(2) 4½" x 12½" (11.4 x 31.8cm) rectangles	(2) 4½" x 17½" (11.4 x 44.5cm) rectangles	(2) 4½" x 12½" (11.4 x 31.8cm) rectangles
	(2) 8" (20.3cm) x WOF strips, subcut:	(1) 8" (20.3cm) x WOF strips, subcut:	(1) 8" (20.3cm) x WOF strips, subcut:
	(6) 8" x 8" (20.3 x 20.3cm) squares	(5) 8" x 8" (20.3 x 20.3cm) squares	(4) 8" x 8" (20.3 x 20.3cm) squares
	(4) 1½" x 1½" (3.8 x 3.8cm) squares	(4) 1½" x 1½" (3.8 x 3.8cm) squares	(4) 1½" x 1½" (3.8 x 3.8cm) squares
	(3) 2" (5.1cm) x WOF strips	(2) 2" (5.1cm) x WOF strips	(2) 2" (5.1cm) x WOF strips
Fabric B	(6) 1½" (3.8cm) x WOF strips, subcut:	(5) 1½" (3.8cm) x WOF strips, subcut:	(5) 1½" (3.8cm) x WOF strips, subcut:
	(4) 1½" x 40½" (3.8 x 102.9cm) strips	(2) 1½" x 40½" (3.8 x 102.9cm) strips	(2) 1½" x 40½" (3.8 x 102.9cm) strips
	(2) 1½" x 15½" (3.8 x 39.4cm) strips	(2) 1½" x 35½" (3.8 x 90.2cm) strips	(2) 1½" x 22½" (3.8 x 57.2cm) strips
	(2) 1½" x 10½" (3.8 x 26.7cm) strips	(2) 1½" x 15½" (3.8 x 39.4cm) strips	(2) 1½" x 15½" (3.8 x 39.8cm) strips
	(1) 8" (20.3cm) x WOF strips, subcut:	(1) 8" (20.3cm) x WOF strips, subcut:	(1) 8" (20.3cm) x WOF strips, subcut:
	(3) 8" x 8" (20.3 x 20.3cm) squares	(3) 8" x 8" (20.3 x 20.3cm) squares	(2) 8" x 8" (20.3 x 20.3cm) squares
	(8) 2½" x 2½" (6.4 x 6.4cm) squares	(8) 2½" x 2½" (6.4 x 6.4cm) squares	(8) 2½" x 2½" (6.4 x 6.4cm) squares
	(3) 3½" x 3½" (8.9 x 8.9cm) squares	(3) 3½" x 3½" (8.9 x 8.9cm) squares	(2) 3½" x 3½" (8.9 x 8.9cm) squares
	(7) 2" (5.1cm) x WOF strips	(5) 2" (5.1cm) x WOF strips	(4) 2" (5.1cm) x WOF strips
	appliqué words, snowflakes, berries	appliqué words, snowflakes, berries	appliqué words, snowflakes, berries
Fabric C	(1) 8" (20.3cm) x WOF strips, subcut:	(1) 8" (20.3cm) x WOF strips, subcut:	(1) 8" (20.3cm) x WOF strips, subcut:
	(3) 8" x 8" (20.3 x 20.3cm) squares	(2) 8" x 8" (20.3 x 20.3cm) squares	(2) 8" x 8" (20.3 x 20.3cm) squares
	(8) 2½" x 2½" (6.4 x 6.4cm) squares	(8) 2½" x 2½" (6.4 x 6.4cm) squares	(8) 2½" x 2½" (6.4 x 6.4cm) squares
	(3) 2" (5.1cm) x WOF strips	(4) 2" (5.1cm) x WOF strips	(3) 2" (5.1cm) x WOF strips
	appliqué leaves	appliqué leaves	appliqué leaves
Fabric D	(1) 3½" (8.9cm) x WOF strips, subcut:	(1) 3½" (8.9cm) x WOF strips, subcut:	(1) 3½" (8.9cm) x WOF strips, subcut:
	(12) 3½" x 3½" (8.9 x 8.9cm) squares	(12) 3½" x 3½" (8.9 x 8.9cm) squares	(8) 3½" x 3½" (8.9 x 8.9cm) squares
	(6) 2" (5.1cm) x WOF strips	(3) 2" (5.1cm) x WOF strips	(3) 2" (5.1cm) x WOF strips
	(1) 20½" (52.1cm) x WOF strips, subcut:	(1) 20½" (52.1cm) x WOF strips, subcut:	(1) 20½" (52.1cm) x WOF strips, subcut:
	(1) 12½" x 20½" (31.8 x 52.1cm) pillow front	(1) 12½" x 20½" (31.8 x 52.1cm) pillow front	(1) 12½" x 20½" (31.8 x 52.1cm) pillow front
	(2) 12½" x 13½" (31.8 x 34.3cm) pillow backs	(2) 12½" x 13½" (31.8 x 34.3cm) pillow backs	(2) 12½" x 13½" (31.8 x 34.3cm) pillow backs
Fabric E	(2) 3½" (8.9cm) x WOF strips, subcut:	(1) 3½" (8.9cm) x WOF strips, subcut:	(1) 3½" (8.9cm) x WOF strips, subcut:
	(15) 3½" x 3½" (8.9 x 8.9cm) squares	(10) 3½" x 3½" (8.9 x 8.9cm) square	(10) 3½" x 3½" (8.9 x 8.9cm) squares
	(1) 18½" (47cm) x WOF strips, subcut:	(1) 18½" (47cm) x WOF strips, subcut:	(1) 18½" (47cm) x WOF strips, subcut:
	(1) 18½" x 18½" (47 x 47cm) pillow front	(1) 18½" x 18½" (47 x 47cm) pillow front	(1) 18½" x 18½" (47 x 47cm) pillow front
	(2) 18½" x 12½" (47 x 31.8cm) pillow backs	(2) 18½" x 12½" (47 x 31.8cm) pillow backs	(2) 18½" x 12½" (47 x 31.8cm) pillow backs
	appliqué leaves	appliqué leaves	appliqué leaves

Making the Blocks

MAKING THE FOUR PATCHES

FOUR PATCH UNITS	
	King
Block 1	(2) WOF strips of Fabric B and C
	Subcut (12) 2" (5.1cm) sections
Block 1 and 2	(4) WOF strips of Fabric B and D
	Subcut (24) 2" (5.1cm) sections
Block 2	(2) WOF strips of Fabric A and D
	Subcut (12) 2" (5.1cm) sections
	Queen
Block 1	(2) WOF strips of Fabric B and C
	Subcut (12) 2" (5.1cm) sections
Block 1 and 2	(4) WOF strips of Fabric B and D
	Subcut (20) 2" (5.1cm) sections
Block 2	(1) WOF strip of Fabric A and D, cut ½
	Subcut (8) 2" (5.1cm) sections
	Full/Twin
Block 1	(1)WOF strip of Fabric B and C, cut ½
	Subcut (8) 2" (5.1cm) sections
Block 1 and 2	(4) WOF strips of Fabric B and D
	Subcut (16) 2" (5.1cm) sections
Block 2	(1) WOF strip of Fabric A and D, cut ½
	Subcut (8) 2" (5.1cm) sections

1. Take two 2" (5.1cm) strips from the Four Patch Units Chart. Sew them together, then press them open. When pressing the strip set open, be careful not to pull or stretch the fabric, and keep the strips straight.

2. As you did with step 1, make a second strip set and press open. Lay one strip set over the other RST with the same fabric colors opposite each other.

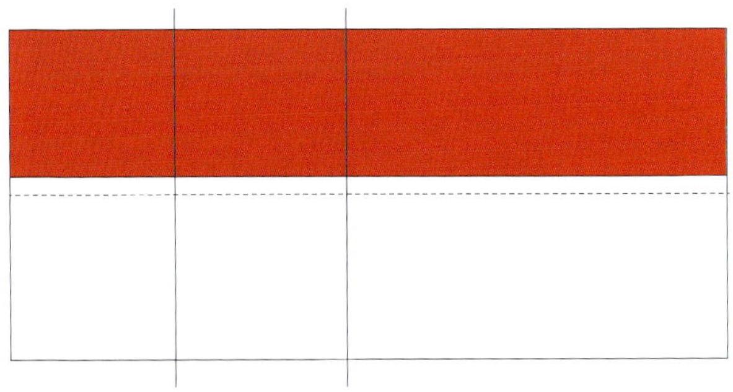

3. Make sure the seams are nested, then cut the 2" (5.1cm) sections for the Four Patch units.

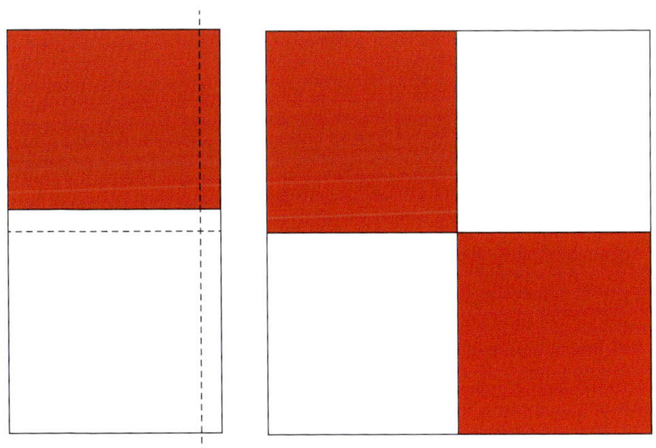

4. Sew each Four Patch section together on the long side, then press open.

5. Continue making strip sets, cutting and sewing the Four Patches needed for the blocks.

MAKING THE RAIL BLOCKS

RAIL BLOCK UNITS	
	King
Block 1	(1) WOF strip of Fabric A and C
	Subcut (12) 3½" (8.9cm) sections
Block 2	(1) WOF strip of Fabric C and B
	Subcut (12) 3½" (8.9cm) sections
	Queen
Block 1	(1) WOF strip of Fabric A and C
	Subcut (12) 3½" (8.9cm) sections
Block 2	(1) WOF strip of Fabric C and B
	Subcut (8) 3½" (8.9cm) sections
	Full/Twin
Block 1	(1) WOF strip of Fabric A and C
	Subcut (8) 3½" (8.9cm) sections
Block 2	(1) WOF strip of Fabric C and B
	Subcut (8) 3½" (8.9cm) sections

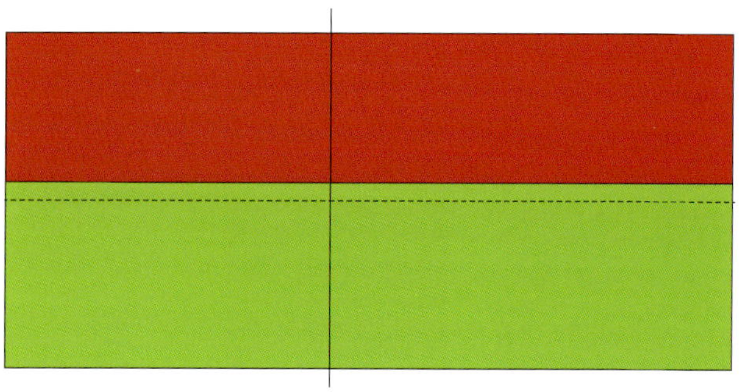

6. Piece just two strips, then cut 3½" (8.9cm) sections to size. Follow the Rail Block Units Chart for the strips sets needed.

MAKING HSTS

HALF-SQUARE TRIANGLE UNITS	
	King
Block 1	(3) 8" x 8" (20.3 x 20.3cm) squares of Fabric A and B
	Make (24) HST units
Block 2	(3) 8" x 8" (20.3 x 20.3cm) squares of Fabric A and C
	Make (24) HST units
	Queen
Block 1	(3) 8" x 8" (20.3 x 20.3cm) squares of Fabric A and B
	Make (24) HST units
Block 2	(3) 8" x 8" (20.3 x 20.3cm) squares of Fabric A and C
	Make (16) HST units
	Full/Twin
Block 1	(2) 8" x 8" (20.3 x 20.3cm) squares of Fabric A and B
	Make (16) HST units
Block 2	(3) 8" x 8" (20.3 x 20.3cm) squares of Fabric A and C
	Make (16) HST units

7. Following the Half-Square Triangle Units Chart, make HSTs. Refer to Half-Square Triangles (page 17) for the Magic 8 Method.

All the units are simple to make, but they combine into a complex block design that will wow your guests!

Assembling the Blocks

Block 1

Block 2

8. Following the diagram for Block 1, sew together the Four Patches, HST units, Rail Blocks, and 3½" x 3½" (8.9 x 8.9cm) Fabric B and D squares. Pay attention to the orientation of each unit. Sew the rows together. Repeat for three blocks total (king), three blocks total (queen), and two blocks total (full/twin).

9. Following the diagram for Block 2, sew together the Four Patches, HST units, Rail Blocks, and 3½" x 3½" (8.9 x 8.9cm) Fabric E squares. Pay attention to the orientation and sew the rows together. Repeat for three blocks total (king), two blocks total (queen), and two blocks total (full/twin).

King

Queen

Full/Twin

10. Sew the blocks together, alternating Block 1 and 2 as in the diagram.

Assembling the Runner

BORDER 1

11. Sew together the following pieces of Fabric B:

- King: (2) 1½" x 40½" (3.8 x 102.9cm) strips and (1) 1½" x 10½" (3.8 x 26.7cm) strip, for a 90½" (229.9cm) strip.
- Queen: (1) 1½" x 40½" (3.8 x 102.9cm) strip and (1) 1½" x 35½" (3.8 x 90.2cm) strip, for a 75½" (191.8cm) strip.
- Full/Twin: (1) 1½" x 40½" (3.8 x 102.9cm) strip (1) 1½" x 22½" (3.8 x 57.2cm) strip, for a 60½" (153.7cm) strip.

12. Repeat step 11. Then sew one Border 1 strip to each side of the runner.

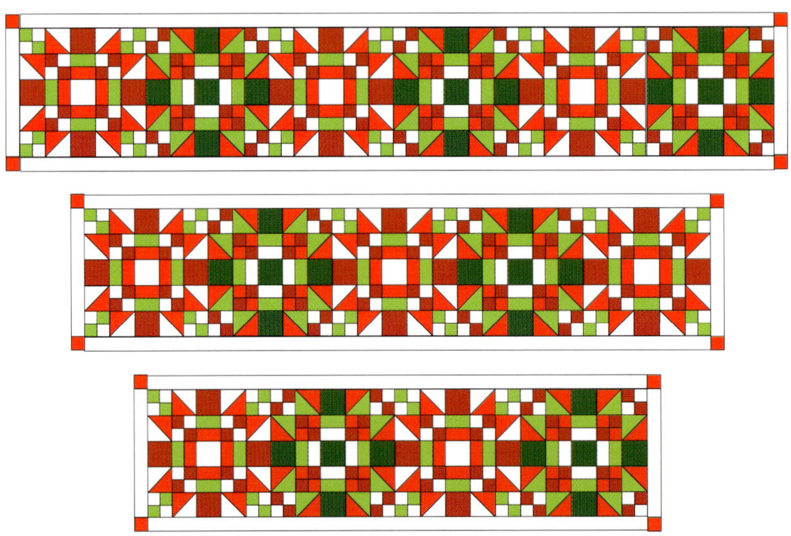

13. Sew a 1½" x 1½" (3.8 x 3.8cm) Fabric A square to each end of a 1½" x 15½" (3.8 x 39.4cm) Fabric B strip. Repeat, and sew one to each end of the runner (all sizes).

BORDER 2

14. Sew together the following pieces of Fabric A:

- King: (2) 4½" x 40½ (11.4 x 102.9cm) strips and (1) 4½" x 12½" (11.4 x 31.8cm) rectangle, for a 92½" (235cm) strip.
- Queen: (1) 4½" x 40½ (11.4 x 102.9cm) strip and (1) 4½" x 37½" (11.4 x 95.3cm) strip, for a 77½" (196.9cm) strip.
- Full/Twin: (1) 4½" x 40½ (11.4 x 102.9cm) strip and (1) 4½" x 12½" (11.4 x 31.8cm) rectangle, for a 52½" (133.4cm) strip.

15. Repeat step 14. Then sew one Border 2 strip to each side of the runner.

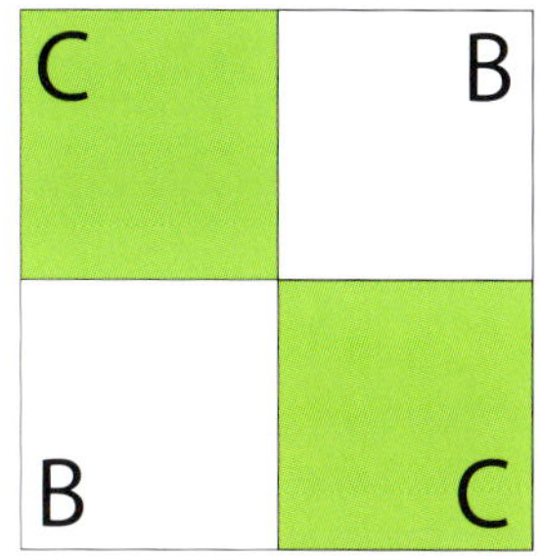

16. Lay out two 2½" x 2½" (6.4 x 6.4cm) Fabric B and C squares in a four patch. Sew the squares into two rows, then sew the rows together to complete one 4½" x 4½" (11.4 x 11.4cm) Four Patch unit. Repeat to make four total Four Patch cornerstones.

17. Sew one of the Four Patch cornerstones to each end of a 4½" x 17½" (11.4 x 44.5cm) Fabric A rectangle. Pay attention to the orientation of the blocks. Repeat, and sew one to each end of the runner (all sizes).

FINISHING

18. Layer the quilt top, batting, and backing. Either hand or machine quilt as desired. If you are using quilting services, leave enough extra on all sides of your batting and backing for your longarmer. Check with them to see what they request for overage.

19. Sew the binding strips together, end to end and at a 45-degree angle. Bind as desired.

Making the Pillows

20. Trace, fuse, and cut out the appliqué pieces for both pillows. Remove the paper backing and position the pieces on the front of the pillows.

21. Using a coordinating thread, appliqué the pieces to the pillow fronts.

22. If you would like to quilt the pillow front before you put on the pillow back, layer the batting and a scrap piece of backing, then quilt your favorite design. You may need to adjust the size of the pillow back if there is any shrinkage caused by the quilting process.

23. On the 12½" (31.8cm) side of 12½" x 13½" (31.8 x 34.3cm) Fabric D rectangle, fold over one edge ½" (1.3cm) toward the wrong side and press. Fold over one more time and press again. Sew carefully along the side of the folded fabric about ⅛" (3.2mm) away from the edge. Repeat with a second Fabric D piece.

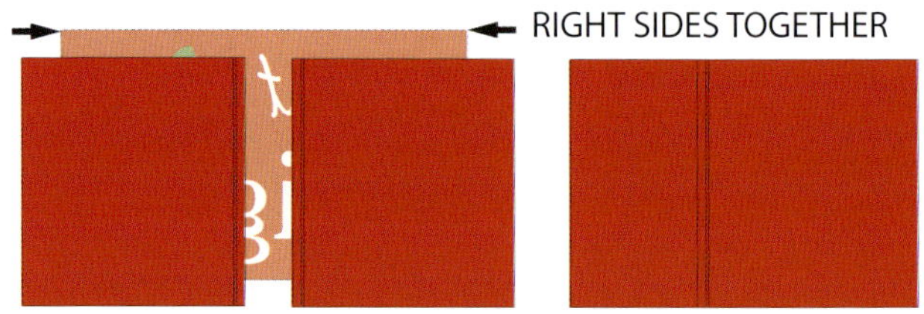

24. Line up the raw edges of each pillow back piece on the pillow front RST. There will be about 5" (12.7cm) overlap. Carefully pin the pieces in place and sew around the entire edge. Trim the excess batting and backing.

25. On the 18½" (47cm) side of 18½" x 12½" (47 x 31.8cm) Fabric G rectangle, fold over one edge ½" (1.3cm) toward the wrong side and press. Fold over one more time and press again. Sew carefully along the side of the folded fabric about ⅛" (3.2mm) away from the edge. Repeat with a second Fabric G piece.

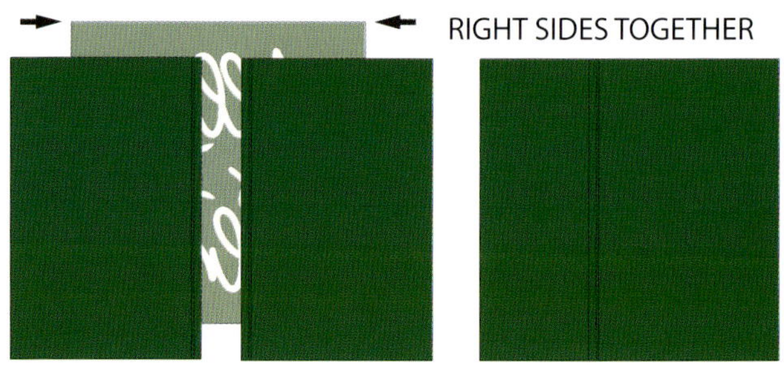

26. Line up the raw edges of each pillow back piece on the pillow front RST. There will be about a 6" (15.2cm) overlap. Carefully pin the edges in place and sew around the entire edge. Trim the excess batting and backing.

27. Turn the pillows right side out and insert the pillow forms.

The bed runner blocks can be made individually and used for pillows. There's so much versatility!

Templates

Winter Friends, page 20
Photocopy at 110%

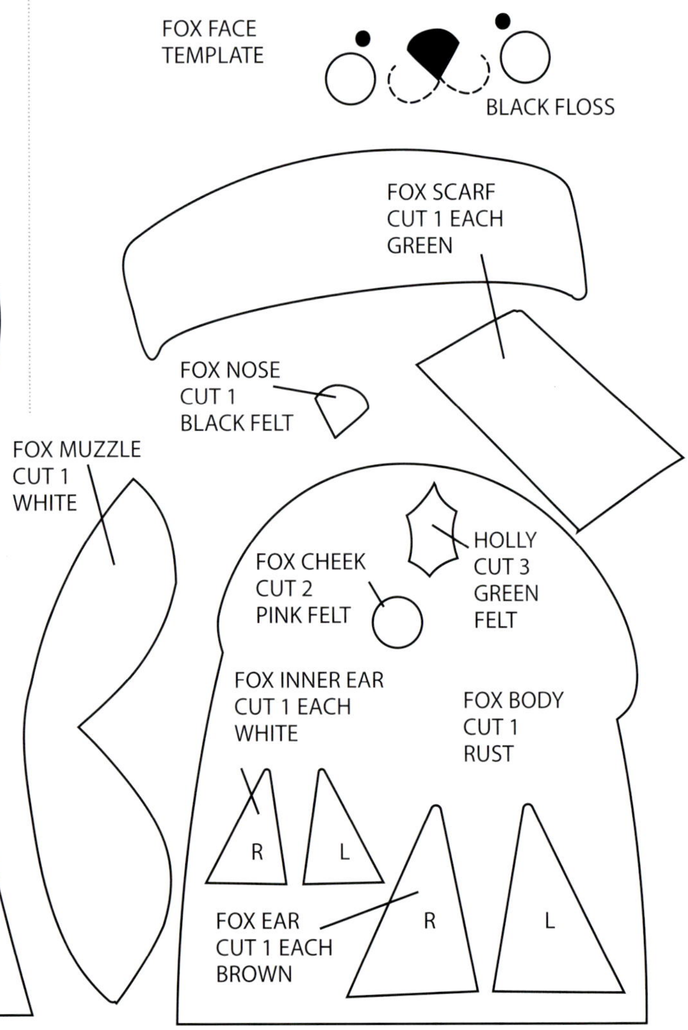

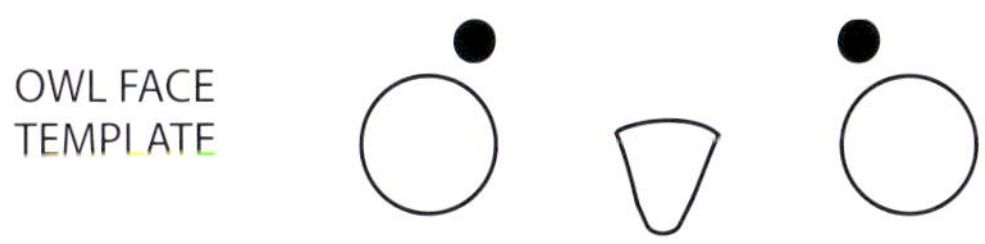
OWL FACE
TEMPLATE

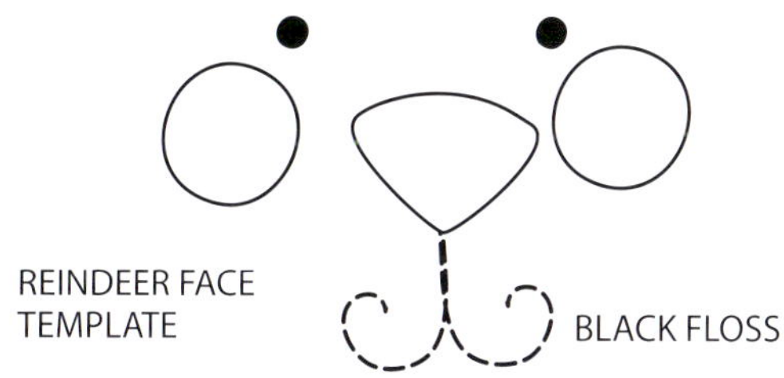
REINDEER FACE
TEMPLATE
BLACK FLOSS

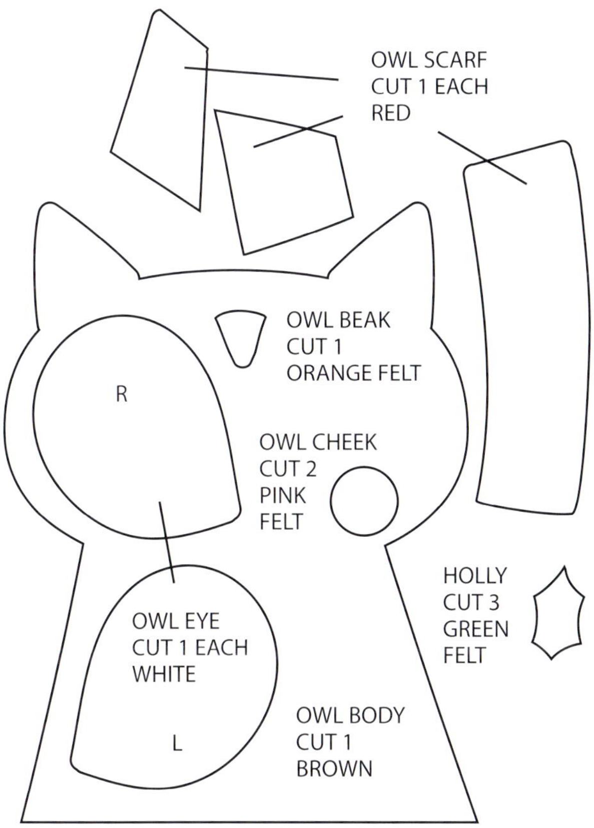
OWL SCARF
CUT 1 EACH
RED
OWL BEAK
CUT 1
ORANGE FELT
R
OWL CHEEK
CUT 2
PINK
FELT
HOLLY
CUT 3
GREEN
FELT
OWL EYE
CUT 1 EACH
WHITE
L
OWL BODY
CUT 1
BROWN

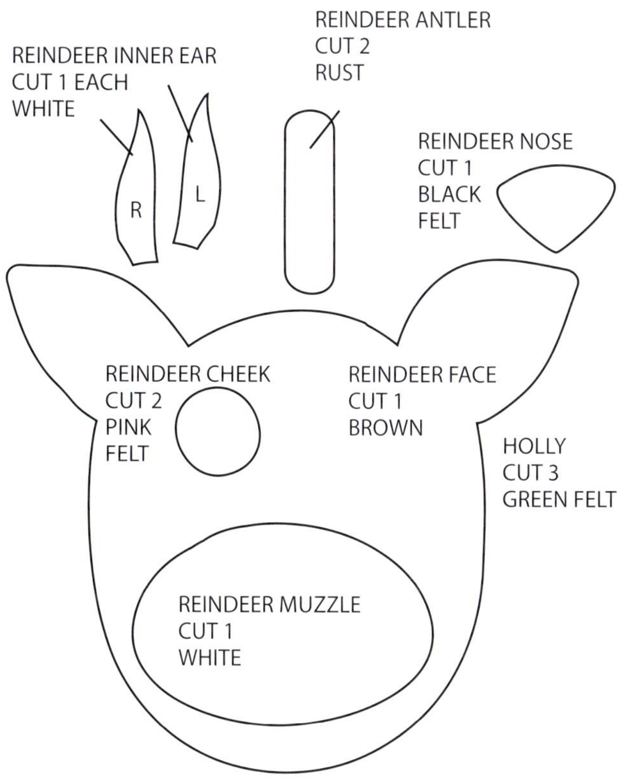
REINDEER ANTLER
CUT 2
RUST
REINDEER INNER EAR
CUT 1 EACH
WHITE
R
L
REINDEER NOSE
CUT 1
BLACK
FELT
REINDEER CHEEK
CUT 2
PINK
FELT
REINDEER FACE
CUT 1
BROWN
HOLLY
CUT 3
GREEN FELT
REINDEER MUZZLE
CUT 1
WHITE

Winter Friends, page 20

Photocopy at 110%

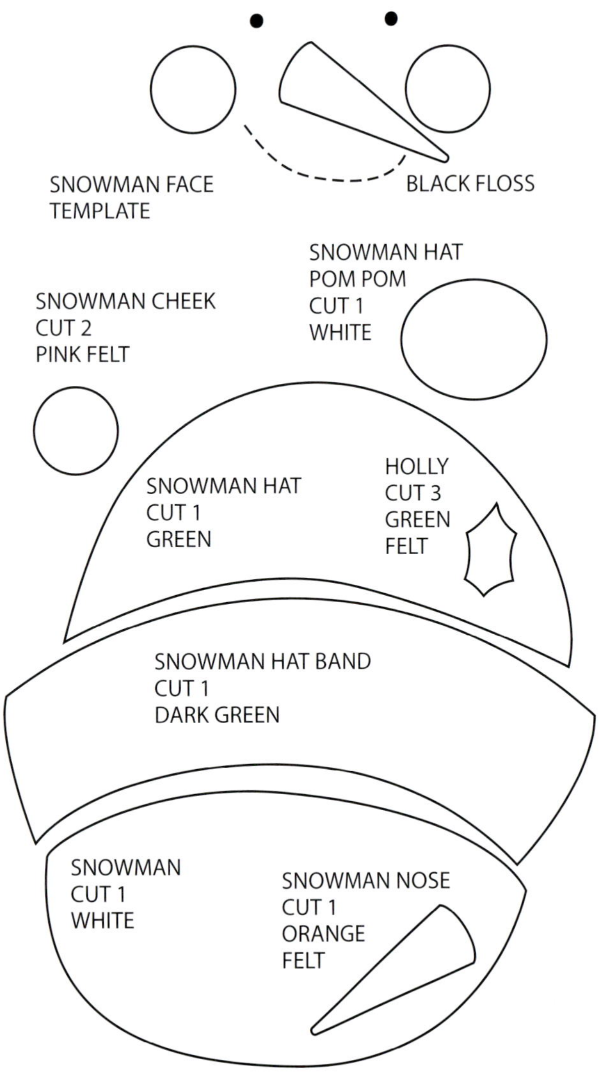

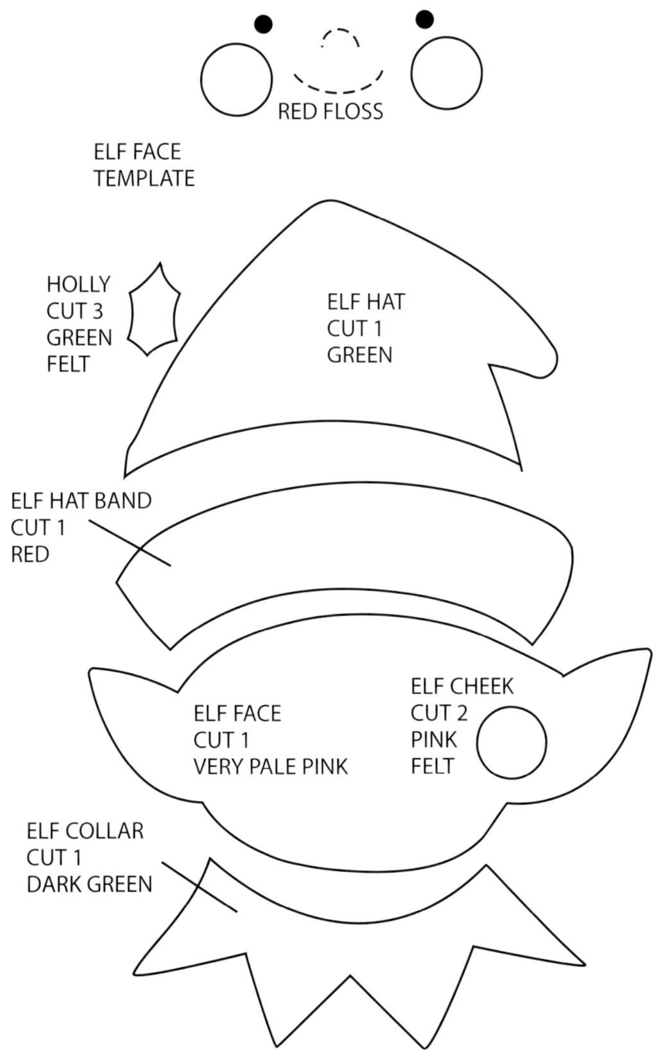

Winter Friends, page 20
Photocopy at 100%

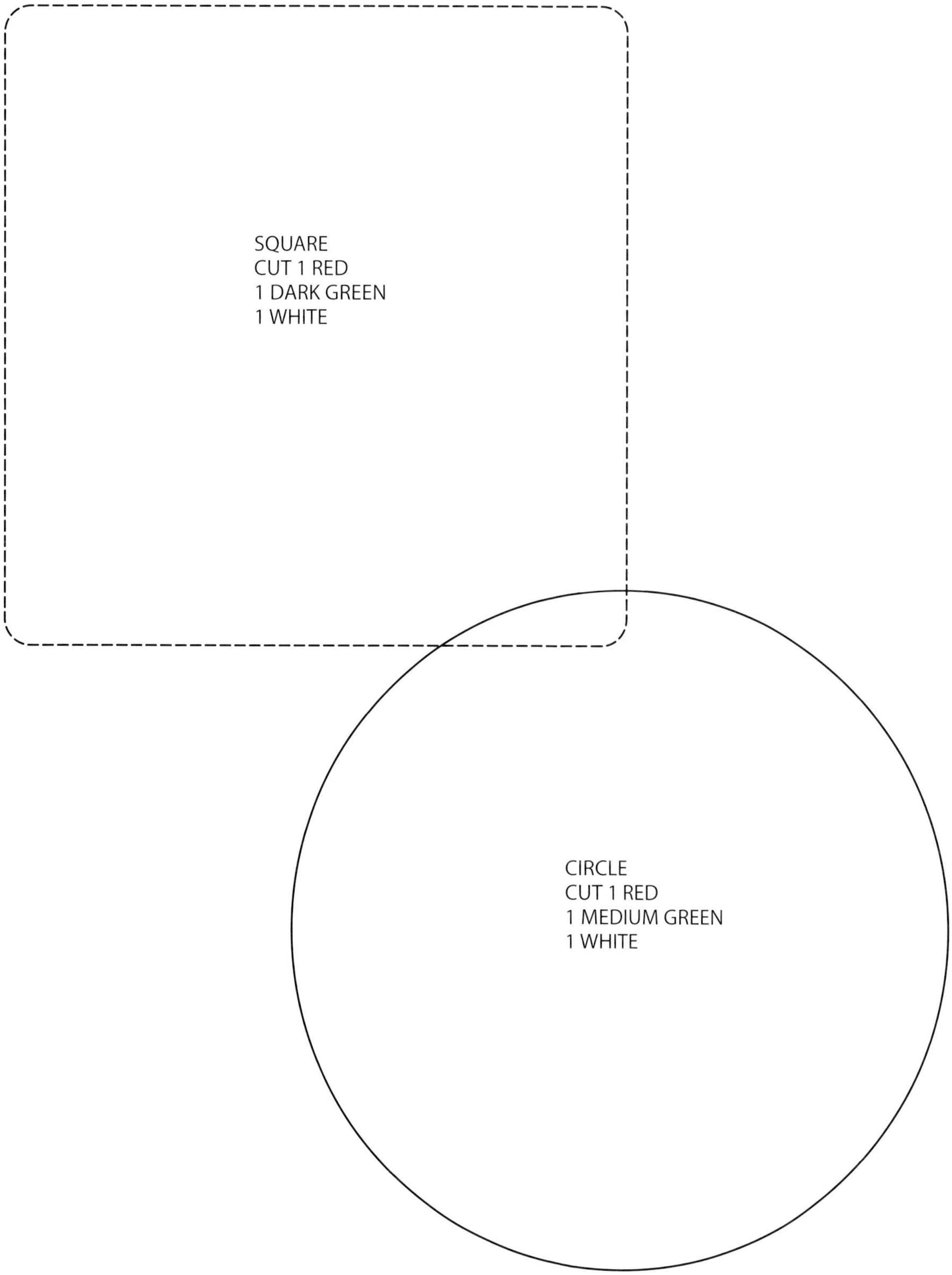

Merry Banner, page 24
Photocopy at 180%

Oh Joy!, page 28
Photocopy at 110%

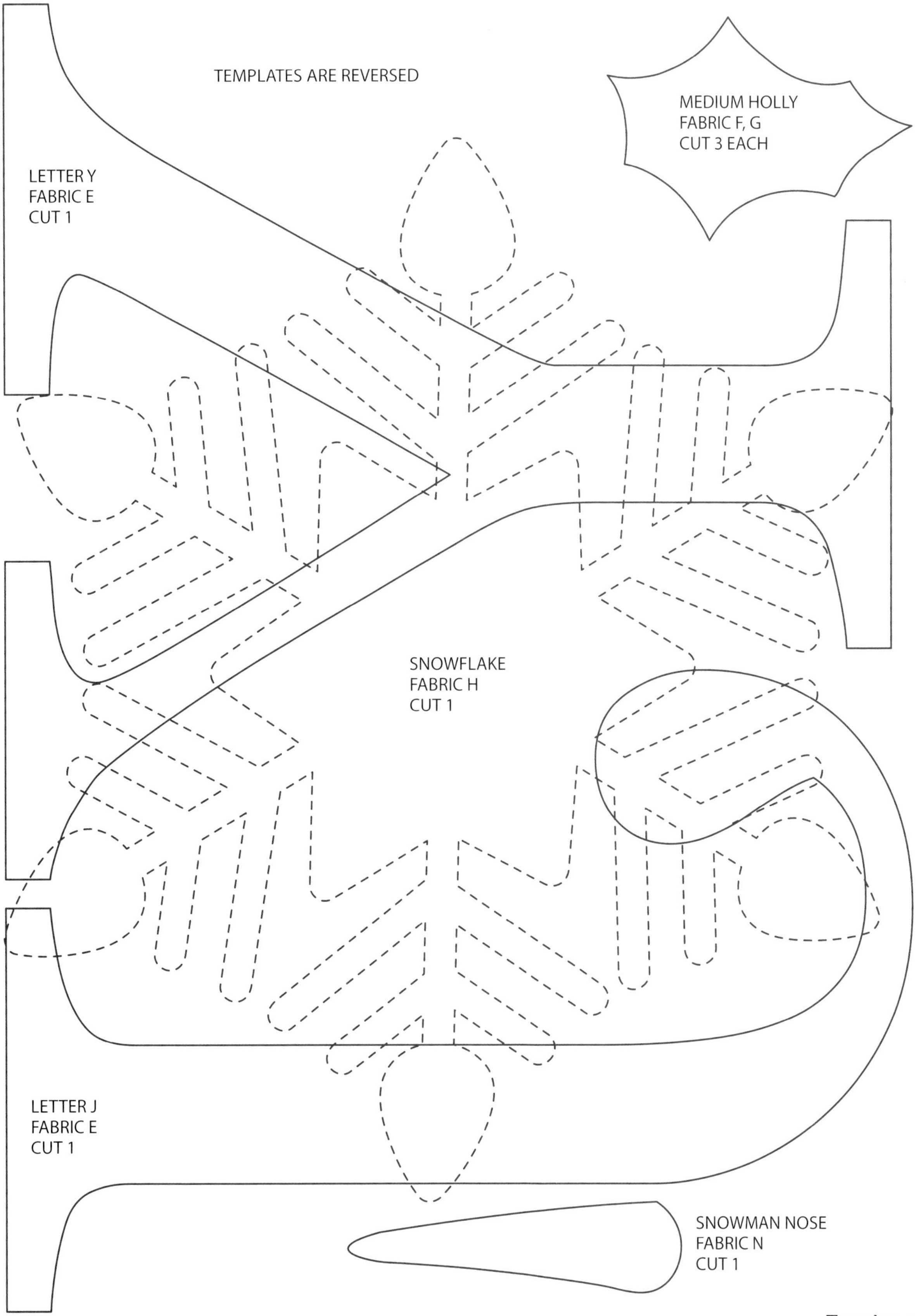

Oh Joy!, page 28
Photocopy at 110%

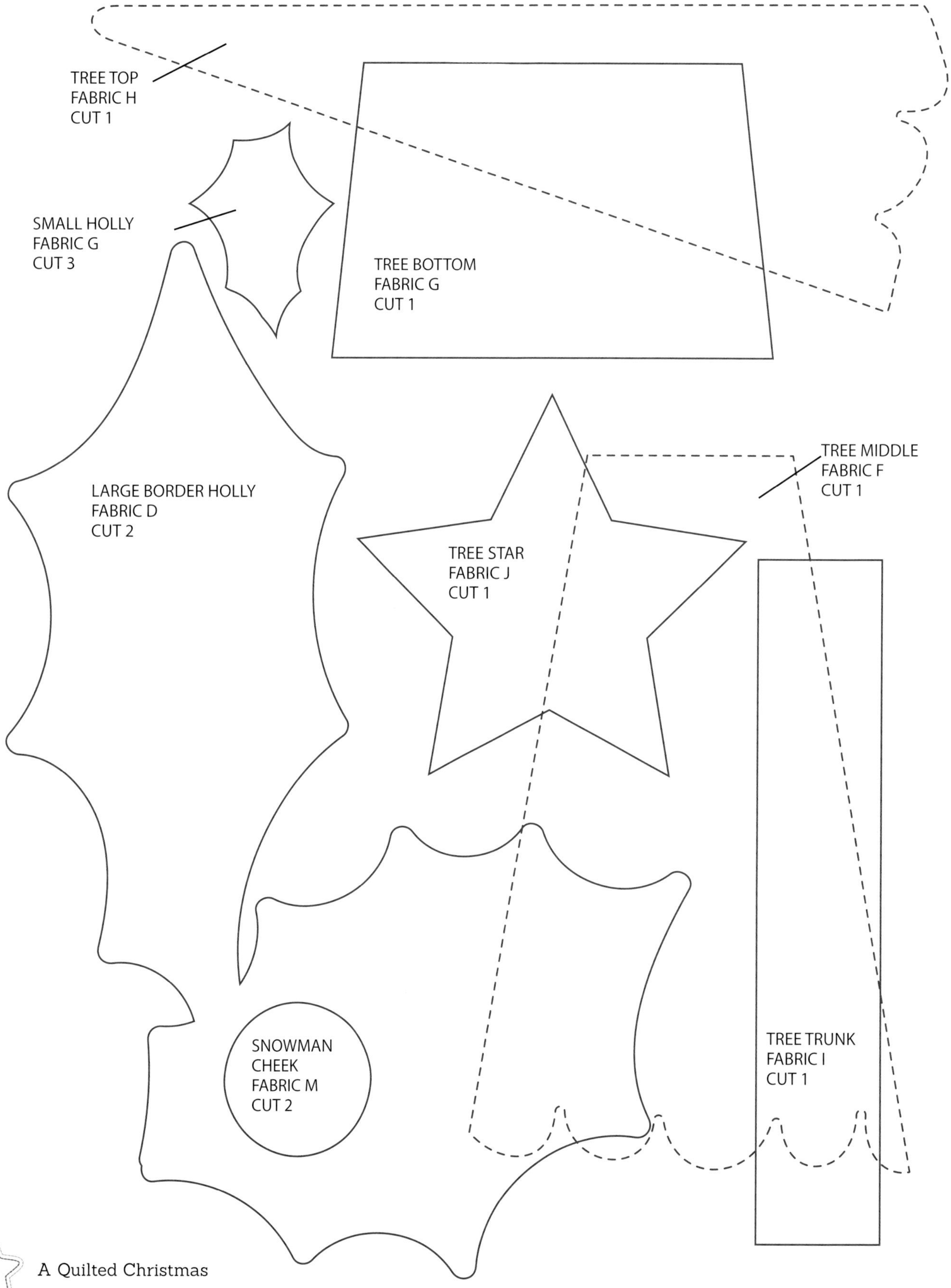

Oh Joy!, page 28
Photocopy at 110%

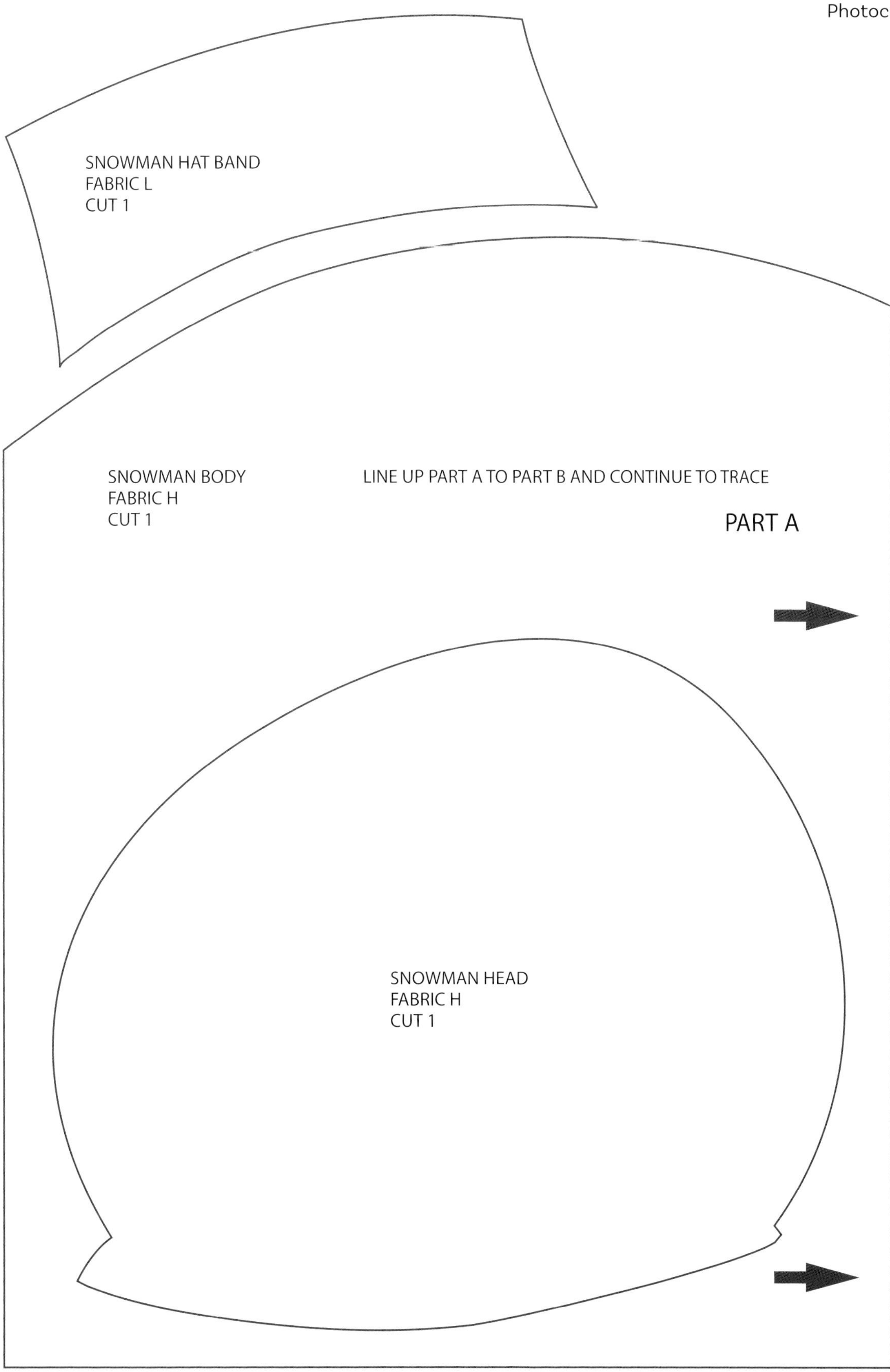

Oh Joy!, page 28
Photocopy at 110%

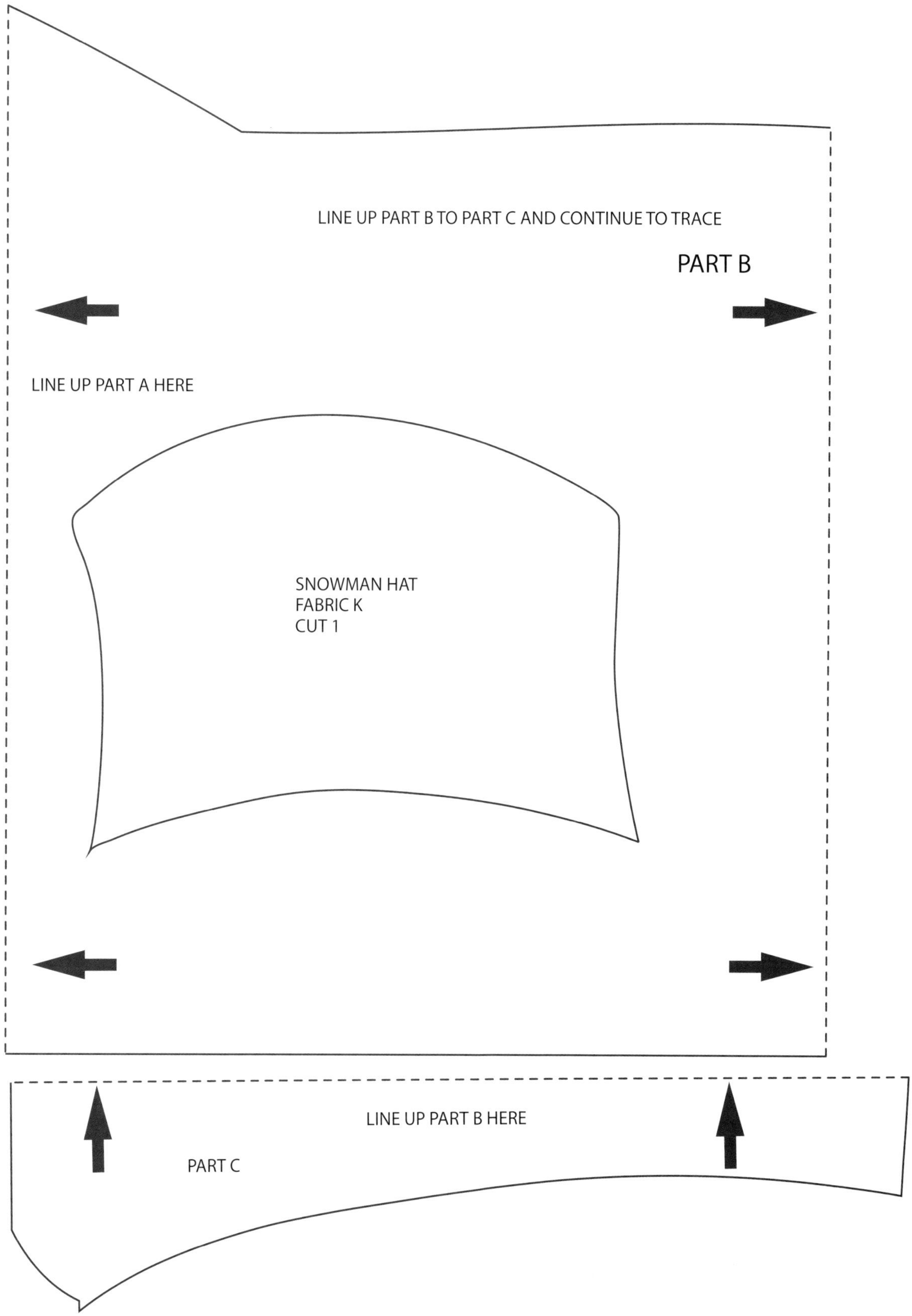

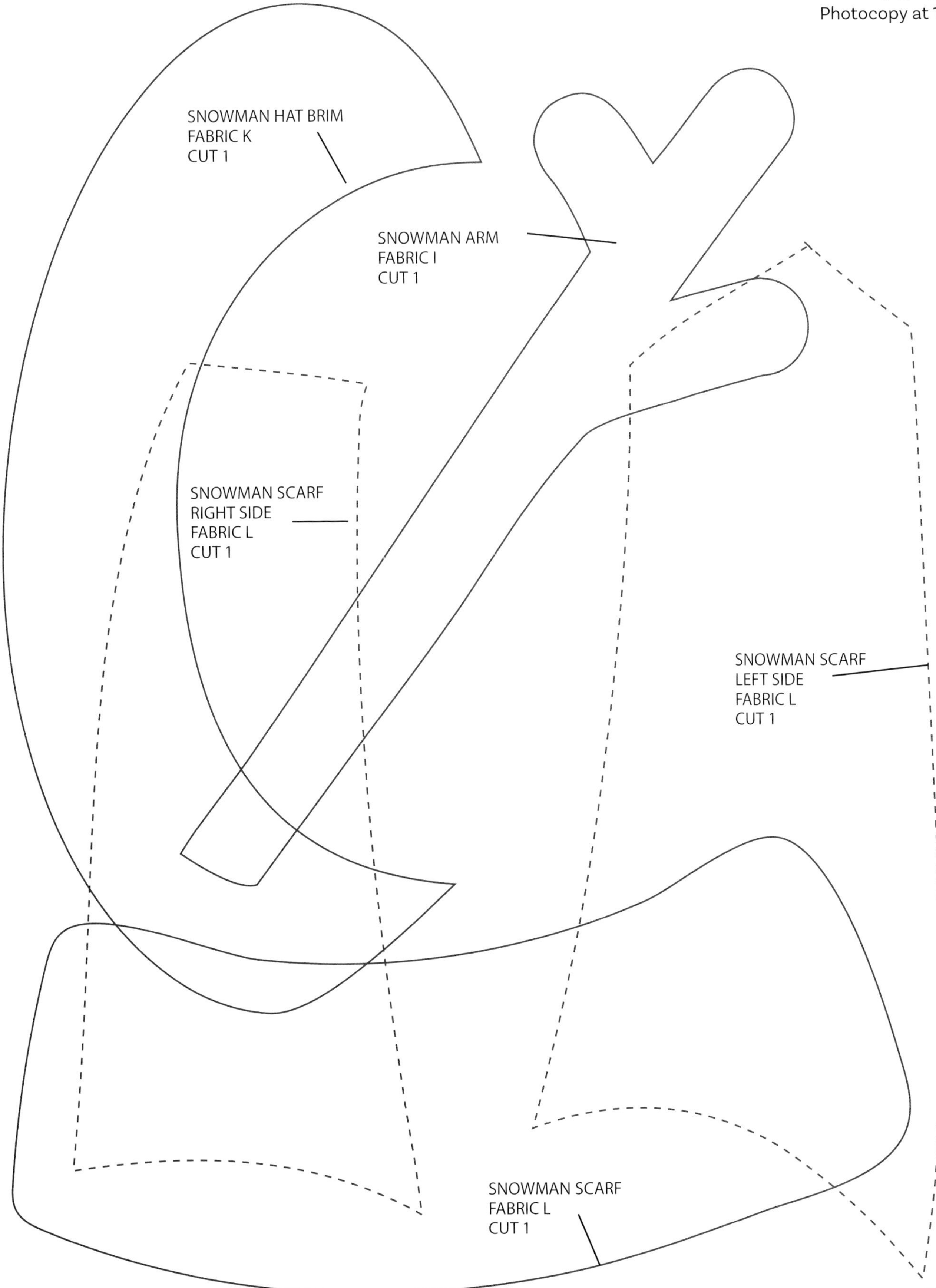
SNOWMAN HAT BRIM
FABRIC K
CUT 1
SNOWMAN ARM
FABRIC I
CUT 1
SNOWMAN SCARF
RIGHT SIDE
FABRIC L
CUT 1
SNOWMAN SCARF
LEFT SIDE
FABRIC L
CUT 1
SNOWMAN SCARF
FABRIC L
CUT 1

Peppermint and Holly, page 36
Photocopy at 100%

LARGE HOLLY
ALL CUT 5
RUNNER CUT 3
PLACEMATS CUT 2

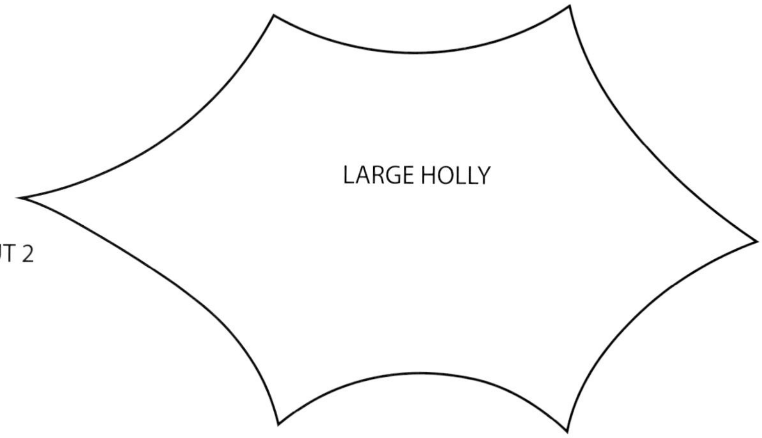

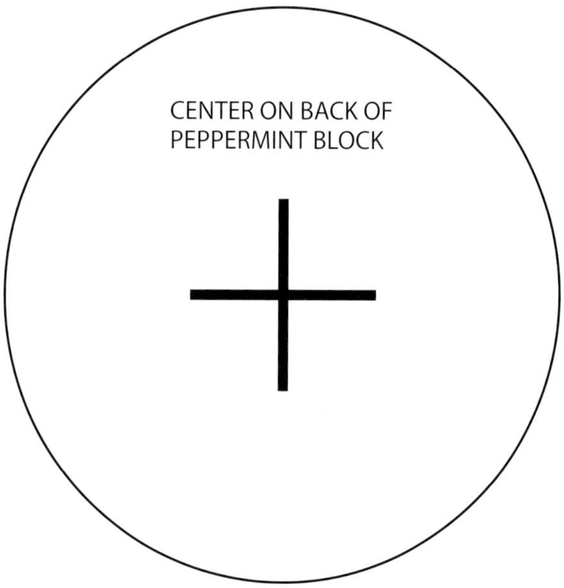

LARGE PEPPERMINT
CUT 6

MEDIUM HOLLY
ALL CUT 21
RUNNER CUT 8
PLACEMATS CUT 8

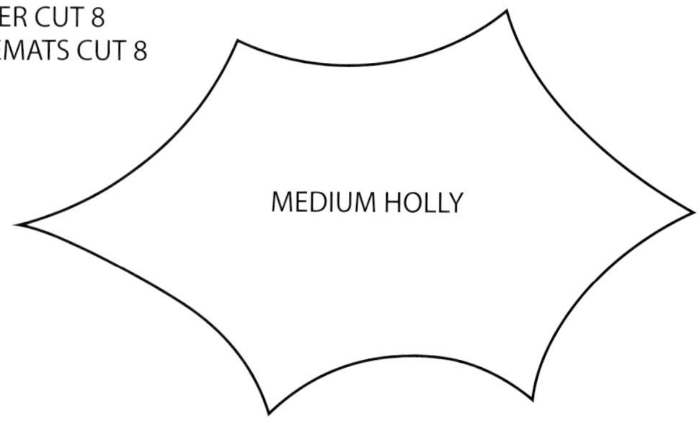

SMALL HOLLY
ALL CUT 16
RUNNER CUT 10
PLACEMATS CUT 4

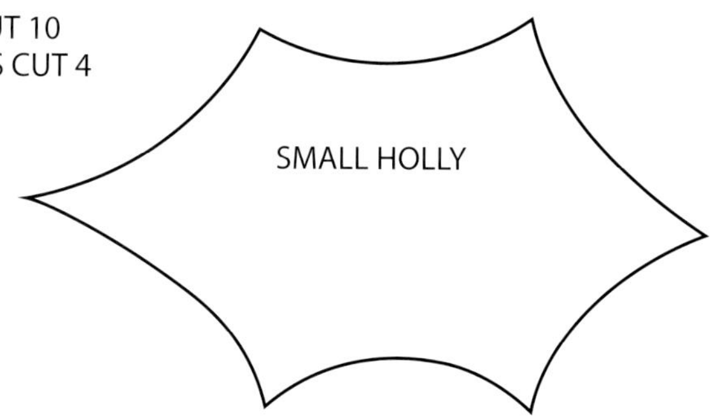

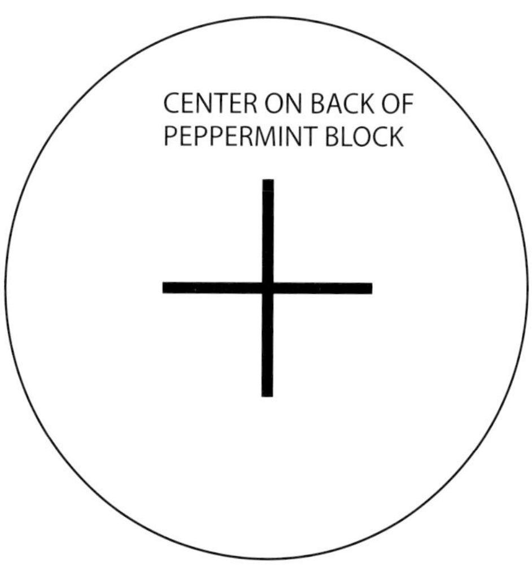

SMALL PEPPERMINT
CUT 14

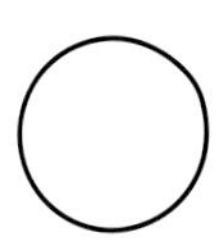

HOLLY BERRY
CUT 38
FABRIC G
CUT 6
FABRIC A

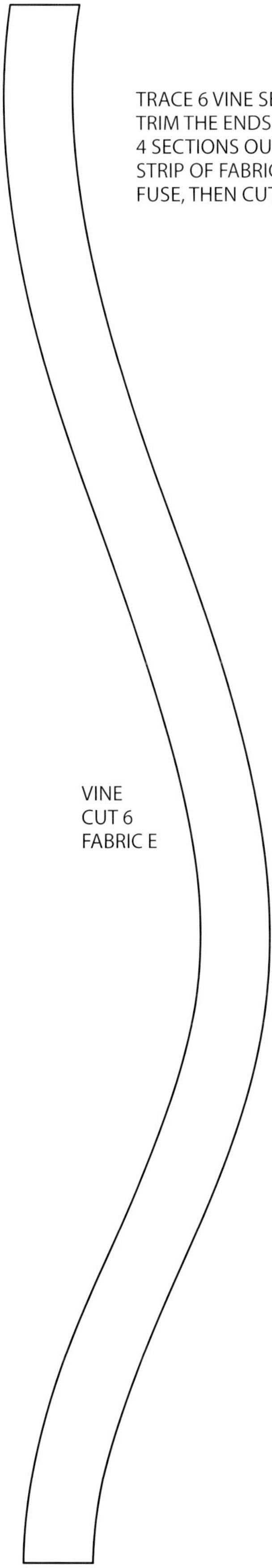

VINE
CUT 6
FABRIC E

TRACE 6 VINE SECTIONS
TRIM THE ENDS AND LAY
4 SECTIONS OUT ON YOUR
STRIP OF FABRIC AS SHOWN
FUSE, THEN CUT OUT

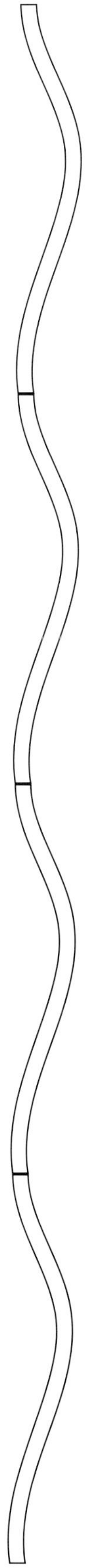

LEFT FACING SPRAY
CUT 6
FABRIC H

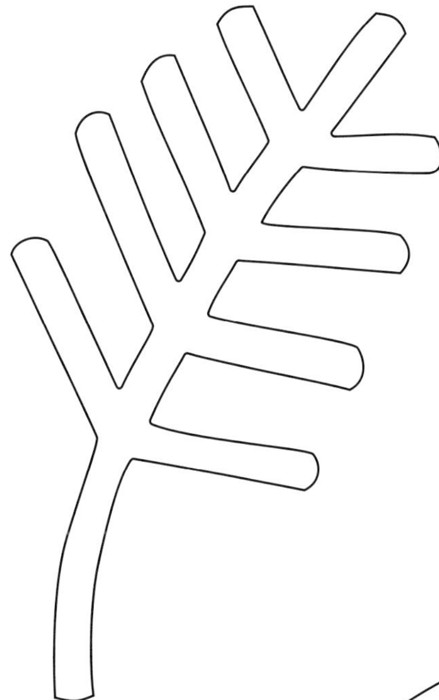

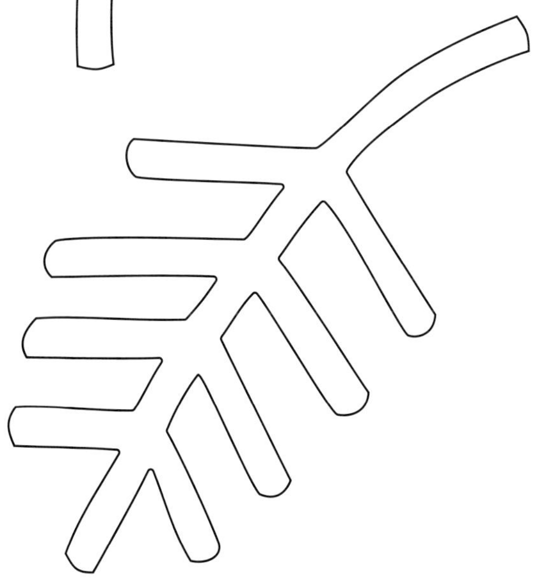

RIGHT FACING SPRAY
CUT 5
FABRIC H

To All a Good Night, page 52

Photocopy at 110%

ALL WORDS
CUT 1 EACH
FABRIC B
PART B

Photocopy at 110%

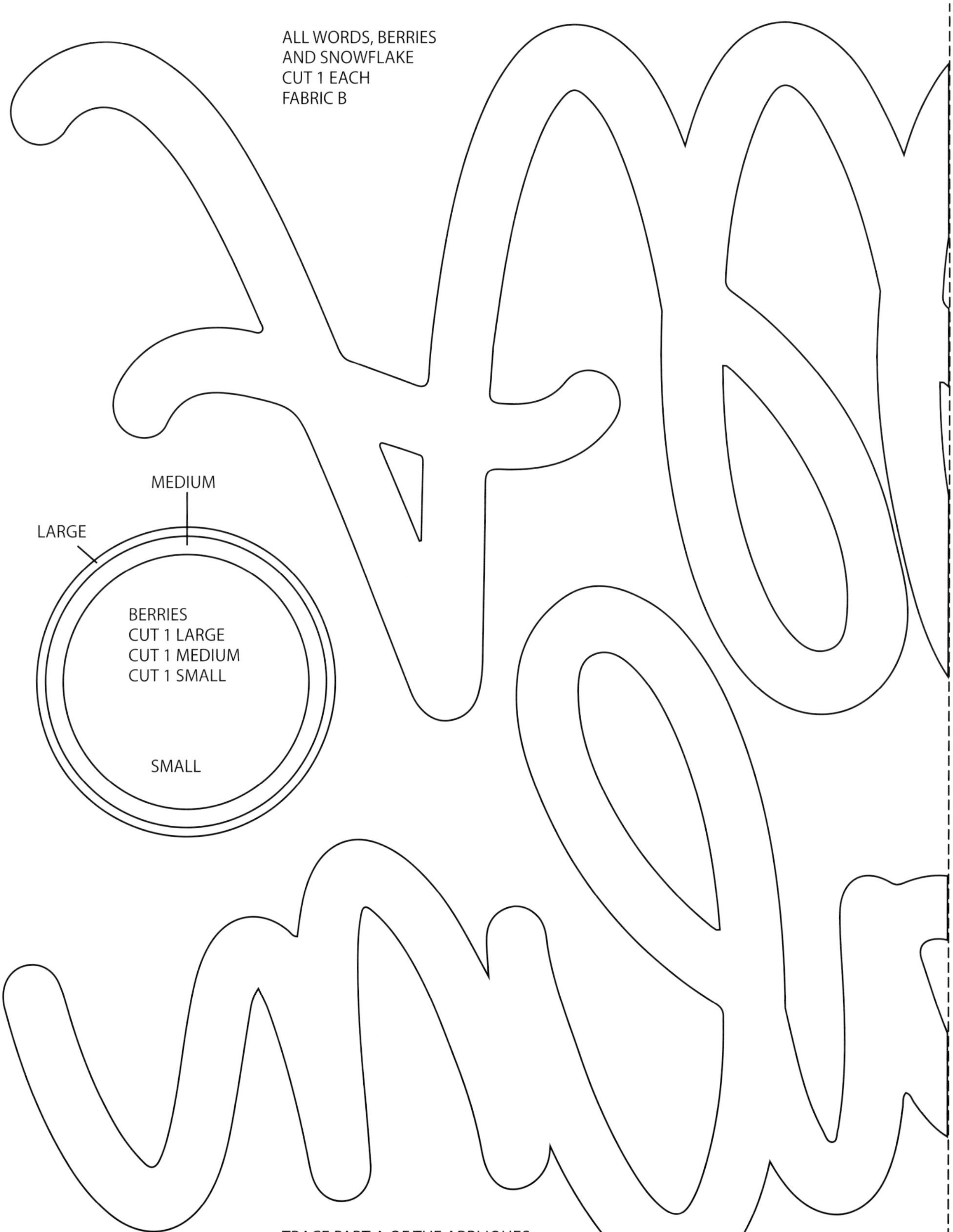

ALL WORDS, BERRIES
AND SNOWFLAKE
CUT 1 EACH
FABRIC B

TRACE THE LEFT SIDE OF THE SNOWFLAKE
THEN TURN YOUR FUSIBLE AROUND AND
TRACE THE TEMPLATE AGAIN TO MAKE
A WHOLE SNOWFLAKE

PART B

Home for the Holidays, page 44
Photocopy at 110%

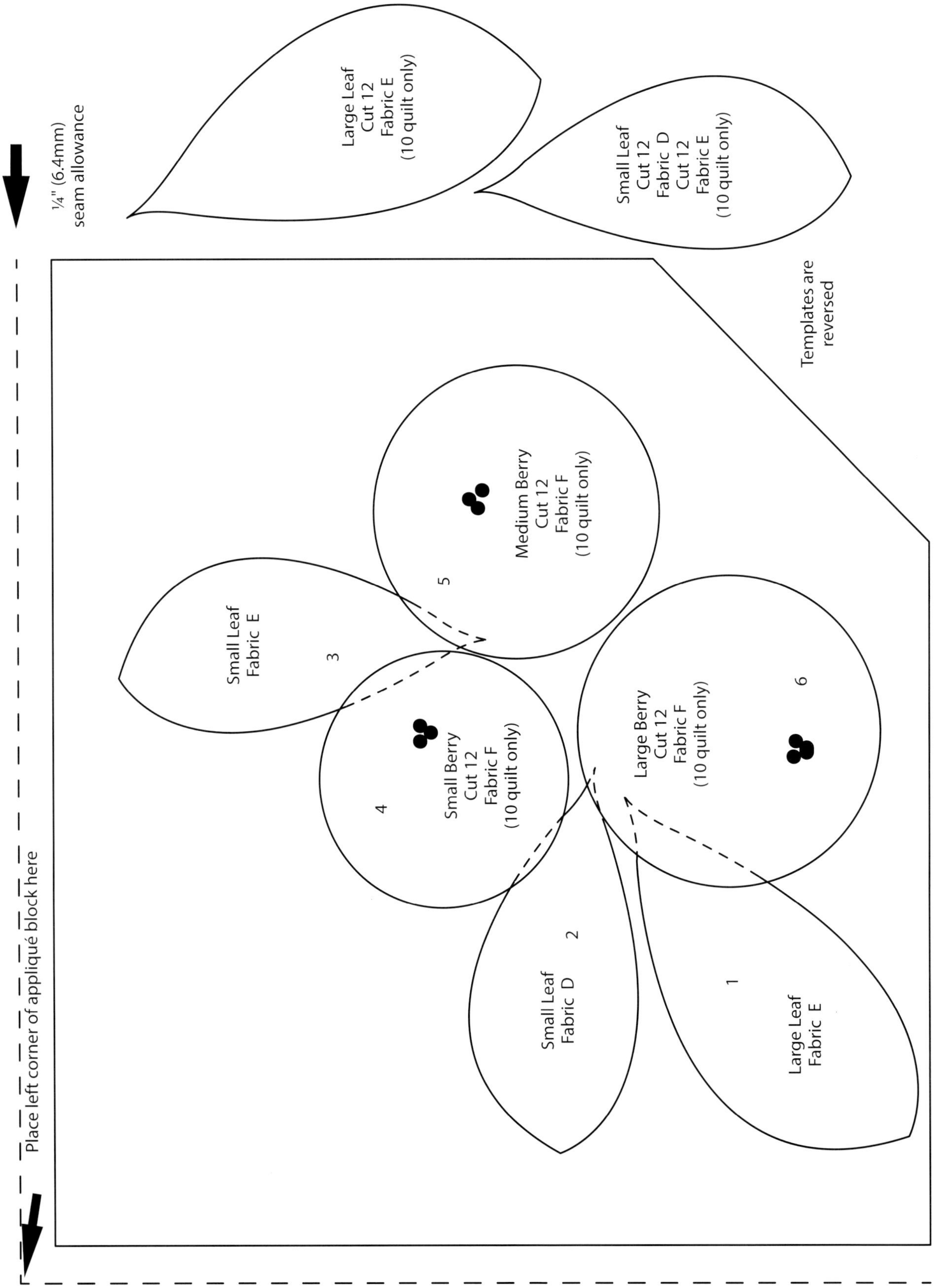

Index

About the Author

As a self-taught quilter, **Deb Grogan** began working with appliqué in her late 30s, using her own art for inspiration. When not quilting in her home studio in Michigan, Deb travels to industry events in Houston and beyond, networking with multiple companies and providing quilt patterns for a variety of quilt projects, from Block of the Month designs to hand embroidery. With over 25 years of experience in art and design, as well as publishing quilt patterns for the past 10 years, she has created a collection of quilt designs available in quilt shops and online.

Acknowledgments

For Anne and Madeline. Together, we are the Musketeers. You have sewn samples and test patterns, including for this book, helped with shows, and so much more. In my personal life, you are my ride-or-die friends, the women who keep me grounded, the ones I don't know what I would do without. Lunch at my house, ladies?

For my husband, Brian, who has supported and believed in every crazy idea I ever had. For every truck loaded and unloaded for a show, all the miles of fabric cut, every pattern folded and packaged, every trip to ship orders, your love and support helped make this all possible.

For Outlaw. Head held high, my friend. Thank you for all your encouragement and mentorship; it was truly life changing.

But mostly, this book is for the quilters. The ladies and gents who buy my patterns, who bought this book, who enjoy my designs, and who continue to support this journey. Thank you for all the love; you all mean the world to me.